# Russian Encounters

## A Memoir

Glenn A. Bever

# Russian Encounters

FIRST EDITION

Book Cover conceptual design by Samuel J. Bever

Cover Photo Images courtesy of NASA

This is a Non-fiction Memoir

Written by Glenn A. Bever

Visit author's website at www.GlennBever.BeverLabs.com

Printed in the United States of America —

First Printing: December 2018

Published by: Tom Bird Retreats, Inc.

Published for: Beverlabs

Hardcover ISBN: 978-1-62747-310-1

Paperback ISBN: 978-1-62747-309-5

Ebook ISBN: 978-1-62747-311-8

"You must be a spy!" the Russian exclaimed.
I laughed and raised my glass. I wasn't worried.
I wasn't a spy and he knew it—I think.

To my wife, Irene. Without her forbearance I could
never have finished this book.

# Acknowledgements

I would like to thank NASA for the many opportunities afforded me during my long career, and my son, Sam Bever, for his conceptual design of my book cover and invaluable advice in editing parts of the book.

# Disclaimer

The views and recollections expressed in this work are mine alone and do not necessarily represent positions of any government, private organization, or other individual. I tell the stories the way I remember them, and in ways they were significant to me. It is not my intent to embarrass anyone other than myself, but as an engineer I am not wired to knowingly fudge the facts, and I apologize if that causes anyone discomfort.

Glenn A. Bever

# Contents

# Preface

This is not a spy novel. It is not a political expose. It is not a romantic intrigue. But my experiences in Russia felt all the more surreal because they were *not* these things. Truth may not have been stranger than the fiction I had grown up with, but it was certainly different.

I am only an engineer, trained to focus on a technical problem until I get it solved, then tweaking it until it is improved enough to get the job done. Then I try developing something new based on a vision I got by working on the previous projects. But I traveled quite a bit over the course of my 42-year career with NASA. I talked with many people and visited many in their homes. I am convinced that if we all knew each other better, we would not be inclined to take our disagreements to the level of nations fighting.

We will disagree. We will bicker; all families do that. But lobbing insults across a great divide, be they of social media, email, newspaper, or hearsay do nothing but *increase* our divides. My experiences illustrate that once people get together to solve a common problem, these differences fall away. What once seemed to be immutable differences suddenly seem abstract and even insignificant. We all want to eat. We all want to protect our families. Most of us want people to get along peacefully. We can individually and collectively do that — if we have the desire to achieve the common goal.

# Prologue: Final Flight

It was Friday, June 10, 2016. I was excited and nervous. My alarm was set for 5:30 a.m., but by 5:15 I couldn't stay in bed any longer. So I got up and went through the normal morning preparations — which in June included killing ants that had found their way into the kitchen. The little beggars just wouldn't get the message that they were not welcome here.

Today was the day I was scheduled to fly an F-15D *Eagle* fighter jet to Mach 2. I had waited a long time for this flight, and now the day was here! NASA Armstrong Flight Operations had scheduled me to occupy the rear seat of NASA #897[1] — a newly repainted aircraft that NASA had obtained from the Air Force. I had been fitted for personal gear and had my egress training. I reassessed what gear I needed to bring today (water — check, pilot log book — check, camera — check, barf bag — check). I drove to the base, listening to the news on the radio to keep my nervousness in check. In the background, my mind played the mantra: *Please don't let me screw up. Please don't let me throw up.*

Arriving at NASA, I took a few minutes to walk around F-15B #837 — an old airplane now on static display by the parking lot. I had worked on that aircraft. A system I designed, the AIMS, was first installed on that plane in 1992 and it was the last aircraft to carry an active AIMS system when it retired in 2009. I contemplated two other aircraft on display that I had worked on — the F-104 and the X-29. For the X-29 I had

---

[1] NASA aircraft are identified by their tail numbers. Aircraft managed by the NASA Armstrong Flight Research Center have three-digit tail numbers starting with the #8.

1

designed a preflight automatic calibration system and on the F-104 Starfighter I had designed a wind shear measurement system. A sister F-104 was the first high-performance aircraft in which I had flown — 35 years before.

I reflected on my 42-year career with NASA. I was grateful for the experience. Working for NASA, I had many and varied opportunities. I had developed laboratory calibration systems and designed microprocessor-based instrumentation for more than a score of NASA research aircraft — and the software to run them. I had flown as a flight test engineer in NASA research aircraft, and I had served as flight director on research flights.

I had progressed into senior management and had acted as Research and Engineering Director, Center Chief Engineer, and even Center Director (for a few days).

Today I was even more grateful that I was in good enough shape at age 63 to be allowed one last flight.

I completed final egress training and then was briefed by the pilot, Troy Asher, on what the flight plan would entail. We would go to Mach 2. We would do a high-speed tower flyby at 75 feet off the deck (ground). We would maneuver. We would request an "Eagle Departure." Yes!

There was a delay in aircraft entry due to a scheduling screw-up, but we finally entered the aircraft and I correctly snapped all the right buckles in the right way. There were a few differences between the actual aircraft and the mockup — such as the oxygen control. I was told to ignore the first switch when ganging them (simultaneously turning several switches on) in an emergency. I had an anxious few moments when I couldn't get the oxygen to feed. Being inexperienced with that aircraft system, I wasn't sure if I had to wait until power was on for the oxygen to feed or if I simply had a switch in the wrong position. It was the latter.

Screw-up number one. (Better redouble my mantra.)

We spent some time doing control checks. Troy wasn't happy with rudder/control surface movement in response to his stick input. It turned out he had neglected to turn a system on — so the electronic augmentation to the manual stick inputs wasn't happening.

*That's why we do preflight checks,* I thought. The test failed due to a system being off — which led to the discovery of the off system (and turning it on).

I stowed my flight bag on the right side where there was a small shelf. It was a tight fit, though, and an aircraft crew member who was helping me situate myself casually suggested I put it on the *left* side — which I did. Troy finished his preflight checks and cranked the engines. The intercom worked, but it was mixed in with radio chatter that contributed to making the intercom nearly unintelligible. Troy called for "clear rails" using hand signals, waving both hands in the direction the canopy would close. Then he lowered and latched the canopy and the noise of the engines became less pronounced.

We taxied to runway 22 and Troy was given permission for an "unrestricted climb" —otherwise known as an "Eagle Departure." The engine power increased and then Troy released the brakes. I was slammed back into my seat as we rolled down the runway with quickly increasing speed. Troy pulled back on the stick. We jumped into the air and shot straight up! We pulled about 4 g, or four times the force of gravity, on that maneuver and my G-suit started to inflate — and continued to inflate. It didn't seem normal to me so I asked Troy if my G-suit should be inflating. He was busy at the time and didn't have time to troubleshoot. Problem was, due to my inexperience I didn't really know if what I was experiencing was normal or not. But my instinct told me it wasn't good.

In a matter of seconds we were levelling off at 20,000 feet. We had rocketed over three miles straight up in that time!

We settled into level flight, and no G's were being pulled — but my suit was *still* inflated.

Definitely not right.

I was being squeezed like a full body blood pressure cuff — and it was getting worse.

"Troy," I gasped. "My G-suit is still inflating. That doesn't seem right."

"Sounds like something is pressing the test button," he said calmly.

I instantly realized what had happened. The G-suit test button is on the left side of the cockpit near the back. When we went vertical, my flight bag slid back and rested on the G-suit test inflation button. I reached back and pulled the bag forward. The suit instantly deflated and I could breathe easily again.

Screw up number two — but at least I recovered.

From then on I made sure my left elbow was lodged on the bag when we maneuvered.

Troy climbed again and levelled out at 45,000 feet when he said "We are in the supersonic corridor. You want to take it?"

*You're damn right I do,* I thought as I acknowledged and assumed control.

"Keep on this course and altitude and bring the throttle up," instructed Troy.

I did.

With Troy calling out Mach numbers, we inched toward Mach 2.[2]

---

[2] At standard temperature for 45,000 feet altitude (-56.5 degrees Celsius), and Mach 2, the true airspeed (TAS) is about 1147 knots or 1320 statute miles per hour (mph). The speed of sound is a function of temperature, which determines the actual airspeed at a given Mach number.

We reached Mach 2.07.

"You have the aircraft," I called to Troy, thereby transferring control of the aircraft back to him so that I could take a picture of the Mach meter. Then he backed off on the throttle.

No change in airspeed.

He backed off more.

The airplane didn't want to slow down. Troy finally had to perform a banking maneuver to slow it subsonic before we reached the end of the supersonic corridor. That maneuver focused sonic energy toward the ground and probably hit Rosamond and Tehachapi with a sonic boom.

Troy then flew to a maneuvering area. He started a series of increasing high-G turns.

3 g ... 4 g ... 5 g ...

As I didn't object, he kept increasing. We maxed out at 5.4 g. That's twice the force of gravity on Jupiter! The G-suit was working and I really did not have any problem with the turns. Without the suit I would likely have blacked out as the force pulled the blood from my head. My effective body weight was nearly 900 pounds! I had a bit more of a problem coming *out* of the turns — experiencing a moment of discomfort in negative G's. He then took the aircraft into a vertical loop. It was a bit disorienting looking up and seeing the ground.

"Do you want to take it and maneuver?" Troy asked.

*You betcha.* I eagerly took control again and made a sweeping right turn, reversed into a left turn, then right again to head back to the base. Troy then took control and did a tower flyby at 75 feet off the deck at 500 knots — which is nearly 600 miles per hour. You really see the speed at that altitude! The ground whips by very quickly. *Yeehah!*

Finally it was time to return to earth. Troy did one touch-and-go followed by a full stop landing.

Not many planes can do Mach 2, and none of them were currently flying, prompting Troy to say, "You are the fastest man in California this month."

Driving home I was still grinning from ear to ear. As I pulled into my driveway at home, I looked forward to seeing the photos taken by the NASA photographer on the ground and seeing what came out of the Go-Pro video camera I had carried onboard. It took a few more hours of bouncing around the house, excitedly telling my family about the experience, before the adrenaline wore off and I crashed.

As I trudged up the stairs to bed, dragging one foot slowly past the other, I thought, "Yep, the fastest man in California ... "

At the time I was born, no airplane was even capable of the speed I flew that day. It is amazing just how far flight has come in the last century. We went from the Wright brothers to supersonic flight in just under 43 years (almost exactly the length of my NASA career). We went to the moon little more than 22 years after that.

I had many experiences at NASA. Among the most interesting were travelling to Europe numerous times to participate in NATO-sponsored activities — and going to Russia nearly 20 times to serve as the on-site engineer representing a combined U.S. government/industry team. These were all interesting and stimulating, but actually *flying* a NASA jet myself: *that* is a rush.

# Part 1: Russia

Part II Essays

# Chapter 1

# It Begins

## The Enemy

Russia. The very name conjures up mysterious activities.

I grew up during the Cold War, which had existed for my entire life. There had never been a time when it wasn't a reality for me. Suddenly in the blink of an eye, it was gone. Who were our enemies? Who were our friends? Where should we be wary? What relationships do we pursue?

All of this was an abstraction to me. The Russians were "over there" behind an "Iron Curtain" that I only got glimpses of. Living in a nation of immigrants, I knew many people from other lands. I also knew many Europeans because I had been to (Western) Europe many times, but I didn't know any Russians. I didn't really understand what life was like in Russia. Russians existed only in occasional news stories — or in fiction.

My whole perspective was about to change.

## NASA Dryden Flight Research Center

The NASA Dryden Flight Research Center is located in the windswept California Mojave Desert about 100 miles north of Los Angeles. Perched next to the large dry lakebed on Edwards Air Force Base, engineers and technicians there have for decades pushed the boundaries of flight. The NASA facility there traces its roots to a contingent of seven people who were sent out from the National Advisory Committee for Aeronautics (NACA) Langley Research Center in Virginia to probe the sound "barrier" with an experimental rocket-powered aircraft designated the X-1. In collaboration with the Army Air Corps, the sound barrier was broken in October of 1946 by Captain Chuck Yeager — a 24-year-old combat ace veteran of World War II.

Muroc Army Airfield, as it was known then, transferred to the U.S. Air Force when that branch was formed in 1947, and then was renamed Edwards Air Force Base after Captain Glen Edwards, a pilot who was killed in an experimental plane crash in 1948.

The NACA High-Speed Flight Station underwent several name changes over the next six decades, including the NASA Flight Research Center, the NASA Hugh L. Dryden Flight Research Center, and finally (in 2014) the NASA Neil A. Armstrong Flight Research Center — after a research test pilot/engineer who worked there (and flew the X-15) before becoming more famous as the first man to walk on the moon.

The Center specialized in flying in the region of the atmosphere between conventional aircraft and spacecraft: high and fast.

When I started work there in 1972, the NASA Flight Research Center — as it was then known — was already well known for several flight milestones other than the first supersonic flight. It was also the home of the first *hypersonic* flight (above Mach 5) — with the rocket-powered X-15. Virtually every other high-speed flight milestone was flown there. The first lifting body (wingless) aircraft was designed, built, and flown there. The first digital fly-by-wire aircraft system was conceived, built, programmed, and flown there. Even low speed — but unworldly — vehicles such as the Lunar Landing Research Vehicle (LLRV), which would train astronauts to land on the moon, were tested there.

During my tenure at that facility, flight research on a wide variety of systems, concepts, and configurations were performed — including advanced flight control, flight effectors, remotely piloted vehicles, aero-elastic materials, advanced instrumentation, winglets, fuel system safety, sonic boom mitigation, and aircraft handling qualities. Many of these technologies have found their way into common usage. Virtually every military and commercial aircraft produced today uses a digital flight-control system. The use of winglets (the upswept ends on wings) is ubiquitous. Even the louvers on top of tractor-trailers on the highway trace their use to testing done on the dry lakebed at Armstrong. The approach and landing tests for the Space Shuttle program were all flown there. The first Space Shuttle returning from space landed there, as did 40% of all the Shuttle landings.

Although I got to participate in many of these projects, the Tu-144LL project stands out as the most unusual one I worked on.

One day in 1994, I was walking down the hall at the NASA Dryden Flight Research Center where I worked, and I was approached by Rich Rood, a fellow instrumentation engineer. He was carrying an armload of books. He smiled; Rich smiled easily.

"Hi, Glenn. They want me to go take a Russian class at the Defense Language Institute and I can't go. Do you want to?" Then he handed me his armload of books, which were Defense Language Institute (DLI) materials.

Next thing I knew, I was on my way to what would be the start of an adventure I could never have imagined.

# Chapter 2

# The Defense Language Institute

In August of 1994 I found myself studying hard at the Defense Language Institute in Monterey, California — where the Department of Defense trained those of high language aptitude to speak, and more importantly, listen to foreign languages. Russian was important because they needed soldiers to listen to radio chatter for intelligence purposes. Of course, now that the Cold War was officially over and the Iron Curtain had fallen, the need for that skill had diminished and the DLI was trying to redefine its mission.

Enter NASA. We had some joint operations going on with Russians on the Mir Space Station and the planned International Space Station. Astronauts would be working closely with, and flying with, the Russian cosmonauts. They needed to learn Russian. NASA contracted with the DLI to provide that training.

Also, NASA was embarking on another type of adventure. We were partnering with Russia in resurrecting one of their supersonic transport aircraft in order to do some flight research with it. The aircraft would be flown in Russia, and the Russians were going to instrument it for us.

Those details were not known to me yet. All I knew was that I was going to the DLI to learn Russian and that I was going to be working on some part of that program.

The NASA Dryden Flight Research Center, my home center, contracted with the DLI to teach two sets of five to six NASA students each over one-month periods. DLI wasn't set up for that. They normally taught Russian to talented, budding linguists over a 46-week period — not a group of engineers (who may or may not be talented linguists) in a *four*-week period. So it was to be a learning experience for everyone.

We had several instructors — all Russians. They each had a different style and focus: grammar, diction, writing, listening comprehension, or vocabulary. One instructor would tell us "Relax. Soak in what you can. Enjoy the experience!"

The next would say "You've got to drill! You've got to drill!"

Class was six or seven hours a day, five days a week. At night we would study. Weekends were free. I *lived* for the weekends.

DLI was on an army post, so we were billeted in the bachelor officers' quarters (BOQ) and ate in the post cafeteria. Monterey is near the coast and is cool and damp. Fog was common. You would also encounter deer on your walks across the post.

So the area was lovely — a big change from the desert in which I lived.

I hated it.

I had never been so depressed. I felt that I was failing — drowning in a sea of Russian. First I had to learn a new alphabet — Cyrillic. (Refer to the appendices to see a listing of the Cyrillic alphabet and some words and phrases.) Then I had to figure out how to write it, as I was told that Russians didn't print. I had a hard time reading the cursive script the instructors wrote. I developed my own printed letters so that I could capture Russian writing in a manner I understood.

Then I had to try to pound in vocabulary, grammar, and — most distressingly — the case system. Russian has six of them and depending on how a word is used in a sentence, the nouns change their endings. This has the advantage of being able to move word order around in a sentence, but it required a lot of retraining the brain. On the other hand, Russian has no definite (the) or indefinite (a/an) articles and omits using the present tense of "to be." For example, whereas in English we might say "I am an engineer," in Russian they would say "I engineer." Fortunately, however, Russian is also quite phonetic. Once you learn how to pronounce the Cyrillic letters you can sound out almost any word.

This skill I did learn and it turned out to be the most useful one to me. I could read the Cyrillic signs in the Moscow Metro, for example, and know where I had to go.

Listening comprehension, though, was a whole other thing. I really felt lost.

One weekend I was really looking forward to halfway through the month was the arrival of my friends Pete and Cindy. They planned to drive up from Palmdale — about six hours away by car — and I relished the thought of spending two blissful days eating out in restaurants and visiting.

A few days before they were to have arrived, however, they let me know they couldn't come. A friend of theirs — a mountain climber — had been killed in Tibet and they had to go to his funeral. Well, I couldn't compete with that. Instead I spent the weekend driving around, trying to decompress.

One consolation I had while I was studying there was that I was not trying to learn Korean. I saw a display in one of the buildings that illustrated it and other languages — and how difficult it was for English-speakers to learn them. They had a scale: category one languages include Spanish and French. German is a category 2. Russian: 3. Korean: 4. I had learned Spanish years before and used it when travelling in Spain.

German I studied some years later. Russian was the hardest for me to learn. It was the most difficult learning exercise I have ever attempted.

After they poured me out of the DLI, I had an overview of the language, had learned the alphabet, and knew some grammar and vocabulary. I was by no means fluent in Russian.

# Chapter 3

# Background

In 1991, the Soviet Union ceased to exist. Overnight, the country that President Reagan called the "evil empire" was no more. Of course, the people were still there. The nations that comprised the Soviet Union were still there. Governments re-formed and the Russian Federation was born. There are many reasons for this shakeup, but the environment at this time was one of an economy in shambles. It was a chaotic time, as people jockeyed for power. One Russian described the environment to me as being like "Chicago in the 1920's." Whereas Moscow had been a pretty safe city to walk around, it was now seeing more street crime. Street muggings. Murder in the subways. Chechen separatists bombing buses. I guess a police state, while making you feel less safe from the police, could make it less likely that petty criminals would accost you.

The Russian Orthodox Church was re-emerging from a long decline. There was a great interest in all things Western: Blue jeans. McDonald's. Packaged products.

The Russian aviation industry was seeing hard times, though. As a result of the new environment, Aeroflot could buy Western aircraft and didn't have to rely on aircraft produced by Russian manufacturers, such as Tupolev. So Tupolev's customer base was drying up and it needed new customers. Into this breach came the proposal to use one of their aircraft to fly the high-speed transport aircraft experiments.

Why was this proposal made? There were really two reasons. One was technical and the other, political. The United States was (once again) interested in developing a supersonic passenger aircraft and Boeing was interested in building one. It would be helpful to collect data on an aircraft of a similar size and speed regime. There were only two candidates: the Concorde and the Tu-144. The Concorde was still in commercial service and had no interest in making one of their aircraft available. The Tu-144, however, was out of service and in fact none were flyable. Politically, the United States was looking for ways to collaborate with Russia on a variety of projects — to help keep them stable. It was an opportunity to build new bridges. Into this environment came the proposal to use the Russian Tu-144 as an experimental test bed. Under the umbrella of the Gore-Chernomyrdin agreement, the Tu-144LL[1] project was born. Advance meetings were held in 1993, and by 1994 the ball was rolling. Work started to get the aircraft flyable and instrumentation installation started in 1995. The first of what would be 27 test flights was flown near the end of 1996 and the last flight was in the spring of 1999.

---

[1] The "LL" designation stands for *Letayushchaya Laboratoriya* (Летающая Лаборатория), which is "flying laboratory" in Russian.

# Chapter 4

# The Russians are Coming

## Hosting Russians

A few months after my DLI experience we hosted a group of Russians both in California and Virginia. This was largely a group of managers and they were accompanied by their interpreter — Sergei Karabonov.

Sergei was a character. He was a young man who was formerly a Russian Army major and had served in the tank corps. (Some months later, during the VE-day celebrating the fiftieth anniversary of the end of World War II in Europe, he took me through several Russian tanks on display in Moscow and filled me in on all the details of their operation.)

He told me that growing up in the Ukraine and Russia, he and all his friends liked to watch James Bond movies.

"We all wanted to be James Bond," he said, "because he got to travel and see interesting places."

Travel outside the Soviet Union was difficult. At one point, Sergei had a job as the interpreter for a Soviet diplomat; this allowed him to visit countries in Western Europe.

He was also a lady's man. He wore a grin under a mustache, and was always making a joke. Somebody once asked him how many languages he spoke.

"One. Russian," he replied, "The rest I interpret!"

When the Russian group arrived in California, we took them directly from the airport to Wilson Vandiver's home in Lancaster, California for a barbeque. They had just gotten off the plane from Russia and traveled an additional two hours by car from LAX to Lancaster. They had been travelling for probably 24 hours by then, but Wilson wanted to treat them to a barbeque in his backyard. Having traveled to Europe a lot myself, I knew how tired they must feel. I felt for them, but Wilson had his own inviting Arkansas charm and they seemed to have a good time.

## Wilson Vandiver

Wilson Vandiver was my predecessor on the program and we overlapped on a number of my early trips to Russia. I had known Wilson for many years — ever since I started at NASA. For years, as a second job, he had driven a bus to work loaded with commuters to NASA. I was one of those commuters, so I spent much time watching him drive. He and I also worked in the same discipline area: flight instrumentation. He was a very affable person, engaging in a down home-sort of way. He was from Arkansas and carried that accent with him throughout his many years in California.

Our approach to problems differed, however. Whereas I would be inclined to mull over a problem and get clear on my issues and questions before calling someone to ask about my concerns, Wilson's first reaction would be to pick up the phone and call. Where this difference in approach crossed the boundary was when I would come to him and express some of my half-formed questions and he would immediately dial someone on the phone and hand it to me. I was then put on the spot and forced to short-circuit my natural reluctance to seek help from unknown people before I felt ready to do so.

Despite our differences in approach — or perhaps because of them — we made a good team. Wilson would set people at ease and I would slide in and cover the details. Wilson never changed. No matter where he was, he was still Wilson and interacted in exactly the same way with people whether in California or Moscow. He was authentic, and that showed through. I wouldn't call Wilson laid-back; he could be very intense, but it came from a relaxed manner that was inoffensive. In short, he was well suited to breaking cultural boundaries and not confusing people with inconsistencies. What you saw is what you got.

Wilson did have his comfort zones, and driving was one of them. Given his bus-driving background, he was very interested in where we were going and how to get there. In Moscow, we always had a Russian driver and vehicle provided by a company called IBP. Our interpreter would meet us at the airport and escort us to the vehicle where we would be driven to our hotel. When we went to the Tupolev Moscow office or the Zhukovsky air base, the driver picked us up and took us. Wilson always wanted to know the details of our route — but communicating with the driver was difficult, if not impossible, given the language barrier. Couple that with the insane driving in Moscow and this was one time Wilson was not relaxed. He would sit rigidly in the back seat, leaning forward, hands placed on the front seat back — with knuckles white. My approach was the opposite. I expressed no interest in our actual routing details. I spent my time observing the people and rolling scenery out the window. I sat back and surrendered myself to the absurdities of Russian traffic.

Many American driving rules baffled the Russians. As we were driving around the Los Angeles area, Sergei was sitting in the back seat and he decided to pop open a can of beer. Wilson was driving and about came unglued.

"You can't open a beer in the car!" he told Sergei with some agitation.

"Why not?" asked Sergei, innocently.

"Because it's illegal! We have an 'open container' law," exclaimed Wilson.

"Why is it illegal? I'm not even driving," said Sergei.

"We can be stopped by the police for having that open beer can in the car."

"What kind of a democracy is this?" asked Sergei.

Later we were driving across the desert and came to a stop sign in the middle of nowhere. Wilson stopped. Sergei looked left. He looked right.

"Why did you stop?" he asked.

"There's a stop sign," Wilson told him. (Duh!)

"But there are no cars coming," Sergei persisted.

"Just because you don't see a car doesn't mean it's not there," Wilson responded.

When I later traveled to Moscow I could understand his confusion about our traffic laws. There it was every man for himself and there was no discernable "social contract" between the drivers. It was reminiscent of the "driving rules of Paris" that I had received some years prior. Here are some of them:

- Green light means "go." Yellow light means "go." Red light means "go if the guy in front of you went."
- The number of traffic lanes is 1 ½ times the number marked. For motorcycles it is two times.
- Sidewalks are for the purpose of parking the car.
- Turn signals will be used to signify the successful completion of a turn.

In Moscow, if the lanes were clogged and the opposing traffic lanes were not, our driver would use them — even if it were a divided road and cars were coming. Not for the faint of heart.

I have driven many places in Europe, from England — even London — to Poland. While driving in those places can be challenging, I never really had a problem doing it. In Moscow I never had any desire to drive. I wasn't up to the challenge.

## Disneyland

We took the Russians to Disneyland, Universal Studios, and the beach. Disneyland used to have a large, open parking lot — before they built "California Adventure" over it. Walking through the parking lot, I pointed to the poles, which had Disney cartoon characters (Goofy, Mickey, Donald Duck, etc.) on them so you could identify where you parked your car. Sergei noted, "That means nothing to us. We don't know these characters."

No mouse ears were worn that day.

## Virginia

The Russians came to the NASA Langley Research Center in Virginia on another trip and I came along to participate and get to know the Russians better. In my hotel room, I was just rolling into bed when I got a call from one of our NASA Langley hosts.

Groggily, I answered the phone and he asked "Do you think the Russians would like to go out on the town tonight?" I looked at the clock — 11 p.m.

"No!" I said crossly, "It's late. They're tired!" and hung up.

Now, I normally had to be at work at Dryden by 7:30 a.m. — a 35-mile commute. The hours are early to take advantage of flying in the calmest part of the day in the California desert, so 11:00 p.m. is way past my bed time. The thought of going "out" at that time was anathema to me, and I knew they had just flown in from Moscow. Maybe I was wrong, but truth be told I knew that *I* didn't want to go out then.

During that visit we took the Russians to Williamsburg, Virginia. The town is configured to simulate Virginia village life in the late 1700s. While no mouse ears were worn at Disneyland, tri-cornered hats were worn by at least one Russian, Mr. Sablev, at Williamsburg.

I couldn't get them in the stocks, however. The Russians were very suspicious of that device. I "took one for the team" and had a photo taken with my head and wrists in the stocks.

# Chapter 5

# In Country

### First Trip to Russia

The day finally arrived for me to go to Russia myself. Wilson was the instrumentation engineer from Dryden assigned to the project. He was going to retire soon, so I went along to facilitate the transition from him to me. We flew on Delta Airlines from LAX through New York to Sheremetyevo Airport in Moscow. It was springtime, and in flying into Sheremetyevo I got my first real look at Russia: Green. Forested. Wet. Moscow loomed and I saw the urban landscape.

I was apprehensive. I didn't know what was coming next. What was the drill after we got off the airplane? I followed the crowd off the jet-way and soon found myself jammed in with hundreds of other passengers waiting to be processed through passport control. It took over an hour but we finally were up. Wilson went first. He didn't seem to have any problem so, relieved, I stepped up. The passport agent was a rather attractive young lady — but grim-faced. She took my papers and checked her list. Then she asked me a question — in Russian. Uh-oh. My Russian skills weren't up to the task. I stared at her blankly and she asked again, somewhat more animated. I was beginning to sweat now. What was going on? Finally she gestured for me to go stand in a circle painted on the floor. I complied, mystified. Was I now in mime prison? As I stood there, watching other passengers be processed through, I racked my brain trying to imagine what the problem was. I knew my passport was good. The Russian visa looked all right to me.

Wilson was long gone. There was a kind of no-man's land past passport control. Nobody is in that zone except for passing through it — one way. I was alone in a strange country without a clue as to what needed to happen to get out of circle hell.

Eventually, I saw Sergei hop over the barrier, talking rapidly as he approached my passport agent's booth. He chattered for a bit and she responded. I was concerned that *he* might get arrested, but figured he knew what he was doing. It was his home turf.

Finally he motioned to me. She nodded, and I, accompanied by Sergei, crossed "Checkpoint Charlie" into Russia — very relieved.

Sergei told me the problem was the spelling of my name on my visa. It was spelled differently than it was on her list. They didn't match. This wasn't really surprising since *neither* one was spelled "correctly" in that they were transliterations of my name from the Latin alphabet (the one we use) into the Cyrillic alphabet. It was a judgment call on the part of whomever made the list and the visa. My name, "Bever," can even be pronounced two different ways in English. The first "e" can be pronounced either long or short. (I use long — as in "fever.") Transliterated into Cyrillic, my name could be spelled two different ways, depending on the pronunciation selected.

Anyway, it saved me having an interpreter meet me at the airport in Moscow. This was to almost always be the case. An interpreter would meet my flight and take me to a van that drove me to my hotel.

## First Flight

The first flight of the Tu-144LL was scheduled to be November 29, 1996. This was the day after American Thanksgiving and was not a day selected by us. Tupolev selected this day and we were not about to ask for a delay, as we had been through a series of Tupolev delays and didn't want to be responsible for another. So, many on the American team, me included, found themselves on a flight to Moscow on Thanksgiving Day, eating Delta "rubber chicken" for Thanksgiving dinner, and arrived, bleary-eyed after 24 hours of travel, the following morning.

We were immediately whisked to the Zhukovsky Air Base, 30 miles by car out of Moscow, to witness the first flight. The Tu-144LL flew a subsonic flight successfully and we were immediately taken to the post-flight party. We were dead on our feet. It's hard to party in that condition, but the Russians were in top form and the toasts continued. The vodka flowed. The tables overflowed with food. All I wanted was a pillow.

The Russian pilots toasted the Tu-144.

"It flies like a good fighter should!" they declared.

Now, Sergei Borisov, the Tupolev chief pilot of the Tu-144, was later invited to Dryden to fly the F-18. He and Dryden pilot Gordon Fullerton flew chase on an SR-71 Blackbird we were testing. (Borisov commented that he had chased an SR-71 once before. "Over the Baltic, and I couldn't catch it.") Borisov said afterwards that the F-18 controls were way too sensitive. After Gordo flew the Tu-144LL, he reported that it "drove like a truck." It was obvious that Russian and American pilots had different expectations regarding how an airplane should handle. They were used to flying aircraft that had different handling criteria.

After a series of flights, I was contacted by Norm Princen, who was the engineer examining handling qualities of the Tu-144LL. He had been examining the flight data and reported a problem with lag in the instrumentation system. "The time

26

between the pilot control input and the aircraft response is too great," he reported. "I need you to find out what the instrumentation system delay is." So I checked into it and found that there was no significant delay. The lag that he noted was due to actual delay between pilot control input and aircraft response. It far exceeded what American standards were. The Tu-144 did, indeed, fly like a truck.

# Chapter 6

# The Tu-144LL Program

The Tu-144LL program was structured so that NASA Langley provided funding from the High Speed Research Program to Boeing, which acted as the prime contractor. Boeing then paid Tupolev Design Bureau (the owner of the Tu-144) through a small British company, IBP, which was owned by an American, to get the Tu-144 flyable and then instrument it to our specifications. Much of the instrumentation was bought by NASA or by Tupolev with money provided by NASA. Boeing then, in essence, sub-contracted to the NASA Dryden Flight Research Center to handle the instrumentation issues on the aircraft. We spent about $700,000 on the instrumentation system. Dryden was responsible for working with Tupolev to come up with the instrumentation list, create calibration equations, collect and record the flight data, troubleshoot the systems, provide the instrumentation itself, transmit the data back to the U.S., and archive it for use by the American team.

The American team was comprised of Boeing, Rockwell, McDonnell Douglas, Pratt & Whitney, and GE. During the program, Boeing bought both Rockwell and McDonnell Douglas, which complicated some things and simplified others.

Tupolev Design Bureau was a Russian "joint stock company" owned by the Russian government in Soviet times, but now was trying to break into the new order by becoming a for-profit company.

## Paint and Rollout

The Tu-144LL program had great visibility in high places since it was unique and represented an early example of Russian-American cooperation. Politically, there was high interest in focusing on a program that was near-term and had quick payback. The Russian Mir space station was flying U.S. astronauts, but it was not a joint design exercise. Burgeoning cooperation in launching the international space station was years away. The Tu-144LL promised to illustrate technical cooperation long before that.

One of the earliest milestones in the project was the aircraft "rollout" ceremony at Zhukovsky air base. Traditionally, this is the point in a development or production activity when an aircraft is rolled out of the hangar and displayed to the admiring crowd — usually amidst great fanfare. The bigger the program, the bigger the ceremony. Often, the ceremony occurs before the aircraft is ready to fly, and the Tu-144LL was no exception.

In the rush to prepare the aircraft for the rollout, Tupolev painted the aircraft, but did such a poor job that the paint was peeling off in large chunks. It had to be repainted with more attention to priming. The engines weren't even mounted. The aircraft was not ready to fly, but cosmetically it was fairly presentable.

The rollout ceremony itself attracted senior managers from all the U.S. companies involved as well as the NASA Acting Associate Administrator of Aeronautics and Space Transportation Technology, Rich Christiansen, who was representing the NASA Administrator. Many of these people we never saw again in Moscow — at least related to the Tu-144LL program. A key figure on site was the U.S. Ambassador to Russia, Thomas Pickering. He and the American leaders occupied the temporary stage built for the festivities. As the worker-bee on the program, I did not.

Another person who was on stage that day was Judith DePaul.

## Judith DePaul

When the Tu-144 flying laboratory (Tu-144LL) project began to form, one of the people who helped pull it together was Judith DePaul. Judith has an interesting background. She was in show business and performed as an opera singer at the New York Metropolitan Opera. She became a producer and produced several musical plays — as well as two Emmy-award winning documentaries. She also was a protégé of Armand Hammer and traveled with him on some of his Russian trips, which created a number of contacts for her in Russia. She formed a small company, based in England, called IBP Aerospace Group and managed to snag a contract with Tupolev that required all companies wanting to do business with Tupolev to pass through her company.

Judith was unique. When she strode into a room, she commanded attention through her charisma. She was a force to be reckoned with. She once told me that as a woman she never broke through the glass ceiling — she landed on top of it. That is a very apt description of her style.

Another large group that arrived and arrayed themselves on stage for the rollout ceremony was the Red Army Choir. This group famously represented the Soviet Union in song and was well known to the West. So it was not a big surprise that they were here, on a former Soviet military base, to sing the praises of the motherland.

What *was* a surprise is when they cut loose, in English, with a rendition of "God Bless America." Standing there taking this in, I had chills running up and down my spine. It was a surreal experience. The enormity of that event struck me, as all of the Cold War years passed before my eyes.

It was a sight and sound I will never forget.

## Chapter 7

# The Russia I Encountered

**Hotel**

While in Moscow, I stayed in one of two hotels: the Radisson or the Renaissance Penta. For my first several trips it was the Radisson, which was an American-owned hotel. It was an adequate place and was near a Metro station. On a few occasions I was not allowed to come to Moscow because the American Vice President, Al Gore, was to be in town. The U.S. Embassy did not want the aggravation of dealing with *us* while they had the V.P. to cater to. I would joke that the Vice President didn't trust other Americans to be around, but a town full of Russians was OK. The Radisson I found to be a bit on the seedy side, so when I was set up in the Penta hotel I didn't complain.

The Penta was a German-owned (Lufthansa) hotel that was very nice — and new. It also sported a NASA business office on the sixth floor, which made contact with the U.S. easier. Were I to use the phone in my room to make a call to the States, it would have cost about seven dollars per minute. My per diem rate for making personal calls was seven dollars per *day*, so calling home would be very expensive if I called for more than one minute. This was in the days before cell phones were ubiquitous.

The business center had phones tied directly to the U.S. via Federal Telecommunication Service (FTS) government lines and had Internet connections, too. This was to be very important to me later as I eventually transmitted flight data back to Dryden via the Internet. It was pretty low speed. The whole of the U.S.

contingent in Moscow shared one T1 link that had a bandwidth (transmission rate) of 1.5 megabits per second. By contrast, my home Internet connection these days is about 50 times that rate. It would literally take all night to transmit one flight's data back to Dryden.

There was only one key to the NASA Business Center. You had to get it at the front desk — on the first floor. Later in the program, technicians from NASA Marshall Space Flight Center wired every room on the sixth floor with an Ethernet connection and FTS phone line. This was heaven! Now I could set up my data transfer in my own room and monitor it throughout the night without having to go to the business center to check it. I needed to periodically monitor the progress of the data transfer because it would sometimes abort the transfer and I would have to start over. Now I could just pop open an eye from my bed and see if things were going OK.

I was essentially a liaison as part of my duties, and much of my work involved emailing project team members back at NASA. Being able to email from my room significantly increased my productivity. I took advantage of the time difference, which was 11 hours between Moscow and California. Only a 12-hour time difference would have been greater in terms of time-of-day (not date). There was no common work day between my home center in California and Moscow. So I would spend the day working in Moscow or Zhukovsky Air Base, then go back to my room and email questions or answers back to the States, go to bed — and by the time I woke up, NASA had worked a full day and provided me with more questions or answers that I could take back to Tupolev.

The Penta had one other perk. Its restaurant was fabulous. There was always a good spread. (I suspect having the hotel owned by a German airline facilitated the supply chain.) I particularly liked breakfast, which was a buffet, and we were serenaded by harpists up in the balcony. Heavenly food. Heavenly chorus. It was expensive, though.

## McDonald's

One of the first Western restaurants to come to Moscow was a McDonald's. When it opened, lines would extend around the block — sometimes more than once. The Russians were fascinated with it. It iconically represented the West and was "exotic." For me it represented a familiar place from home and I decided to go there.

When I arrived, it was crowded. *Great!* I thought. *This will give me time to figure out how things work here and time to decipher the menu.* However, as soon as I squeezed in the door, a McDonald's cashier started waving at me, indicating that her station was open. And it was, incredibly. All the people milling around the counter were not in line. So I just strolled up and took a chance, since I didn't have time to figure out how to order in Russian.

I said "Big Mac," and she punched a button on the register.

On it I saw the word "Big Mac" — in Cyrillic.

So I said "Coke" — and lo and behold the word "Coke" appeared in Cyrillic also.

Not a translation, mind you: an actual transliteration of the word from English into Russian. Easy. Later, when I had a chance to look over the posted menu, *everything* on it was treated the same way. No knowledge of Russian necessary to order. I mean, how *would* you translate "Big Mac" into Russian? I had observed something very similar in a McDonald's restaurant in France, where many of the menu items were listed in English — or maybe English words spelled as the French might to keep the pronunciation similar to English.

Periodically I would dine out at other places in Moscow. I was not very adventurous and was reluctant to eat in a Russian restaurant without guidance, and we seldom dined out with our Russian interpreters. We had plenty of Russian food served to us at Zhukovsky in the cafeteria there, but going out on my own didn't feel safe — and the sanitation was problematic. I mean, watching food being cooked and served on the street in garbage cans didn't help assuage my concerns.

So that left dining in Western restaurants, if you could find them. Following McDonald's success, other familiar restaurants started popping up in Moscow: T.G.I. Friday's, Planet Hollywood, Pizza Hut — all spelled in Cyrillic phonetically matching the English pronunciation. They enjoyed varying degrees of popularity, but not to the degree that McDonald's did. For example, Planet Hollywood sent people to pass out flyers on the street. Arnold Schwarzenegger (who was one of the owners) came to Moscow to draw attention to the place.

But these restaurants were expensive and the average Russian couldn't afford them, so I suspect the patronage was largely expatriates or Western travelers who came out of curiosity —like I did.

The mayor of Moscow noticed that MacDonald's was doing well and decided that Moscow needed fast-food places that were quintessentially Russian. So places started popping up that had as main staples both *Piroshki* and *Kvass*. Piroshki are burrito-sized wraps containing different fillings — such as cabbage and meat. Kvass is a fermented drink commonly made from rye bread. It is very weakly alcoholic (less than 1%) and isn't classified as an alcoholic beverage.

The costs of these were very low — much cheaper than McDonald's hamburgers and soft drinks. The average Russian could afford to buy them. I had them a few times and found them to be quite good.

## Cafeteria

We often ate in the Zhukovsky cafeteria, too. They usually gave us a separate room so that our team could eat together semi-privately. The cook also served our meals, which were usually very good. She obviously wanted to please us and was very solicitous. Russians know how to cook chicken and potatoes. Those were always good. However, there were other foods that were foreign to my palate. Being served a full plate of shredded raw onion was common.

Once the cook, hovering, asked me "Don't you like it?"

I had eaten very little of it. I smiled and said, "I like it. It doesn't like me."

Apparently that translated and she was not offended. Caviar was commonly served. So were liver and beets.

Once the Russians were talking about the strange Asian foods they had encountered and how odd they were. I listened to their discussion with amusement, considering that I was at that moment staring at a table full of foods I didn't know what to do with.

## Stalin Buildings

Prominent features of the Moscow skyline are some skyscrapers that reminded me of the Empire State Building in New York. They had that sort of "period" look about them in their style. They weren't boxy, but rather were tapered toward the top. The story of their creation is interesting, too.

It seems that when the architects drew up plans for the buildings under Joseph Stalin's direction, they drew a couple of different styles for Stalin's approval. They split the building in half on the drawing and sketched up one style of windows on one side and another style on the other. They then included a signature line on both sides with the intent that Stalin would sign one or the other to signify which style he preferred. Unfortunately, apparently nobody told him this was how plans were drawn.

Stalin signed both sides of the drawing.

Nobody had the nerve to point out to Stalin his mistake — so they built the building that way!

As we drove past the buildings, as we did most days, I looked closely at them and could see two distinctly different styles of windows on opposite sides.

A few years later I had occasion to actually go inside one of them. I had been attending non-denominational church services in Moscow that were primarily for the benefit of Westerners in Moscow. The services were held in office buildings, which had room on Sundays. I would take the Metro across town to wherever the services were held. (They moved from time to time.) Many Russians would attend these services as well, in order to practice their English. I attended to touch base with other Americans — a bit of home, as it were.

Among the people I met were a young American couple who were living in Moscow. They invited a group of us to their apartment after church one day, and to my delight I discovered that they lived in one of the Stalin buildings. Knowing the story of their creation enhanced the experience.

## Expensive

Moscow was one of the most expensive cities in the world for foreigners. Moscow had a two-tier price structure for many places. Museums, for example, might charge ten dollars for foreigners and 50 cents for a Muscovite.

Once when my interpreter took me to a museum, he said, "You look Russian. Don't say anything," and he bought me a local ticket.

After several trips to Moscow, and seeing how expensive it was for foreigners, I discovered that you could rent apartments from locals for a fraction of the cost of a hotel. There was at least one catch — you had to pay cash. So I went to the NASA Dryden legal office and asked them about doing this.

The paralegal looked at me and said "Don't try to save the government money. It confuses them." So I dropped it.

It was just as well, because much of my job required access to government telecommunications systems that would have been unavailable to me in a local's apartment.

## U2

As time went on and I had several trips under my belt, they let me off the leash and I often went about Moscow by myself — without an interpreter. On one museum excursion, I found myself in a museum that had many artifacts. They charge you more if you take a camera in, so I left mine — not thinking to find anything photo-worthy.

I was wrong. On an upper floor of the museum I spotted a pile of junk in the corner. Looking more closely I saw U.S. markings on it. When I tested my understanding of Russian by reading the display information I realized that it was Francis Gary Power's U2! This was one of the most famous spying case of the 20th century — one that embarrassed President Eisenhower and imprisoned Powers. Here in Moscow his airplane was displayed obscurely as a pile of wreckage in the corner of a little-known museum.

## Infrastructure

When I first arrived in Moscow and went to Tupolev headquarters there, I was "impressed" by the facility. It was in abysmal shape. The elevators groaned and creaked and to get them started you had to stand around the outside edges so that the load sensors in the floor would not prevent you from ascending. Then they would stop a foot or more below the floor when the doors opened — and you would literally climb out. Most of the lights in the hallway were broken, so the halls were very dark. This was especially bad because there were dogs roaming the halls and they left "presents" everywhere.

Zhukovsky airbase was also suffering from infrastructure problems. The roads to the base from Moscow were littered with potholes. I only encountered one working telephone on the base, and we had to walk several buildings away and up some flights of stairs to get to it. Even calling Moscow from that phone yielded a bad line — noisy, scratchy, and prone to drop. Boeing had hired a Russian to be their liaison and they issued him a cell phone. He was the most popular guy on site because people wanted to use his phone to call Moscow.

The first time I arrived at Zhukovsky, I asked where I could go to the bathroom. They pointed me to the woods. I found out why later when I visited a restroom. It was in ghastly shape. No lights worked and neither did the plumbing. The place was filthy. It was consistent with the rest of the infrastructure problems.

Zhukovsky is located in a forested area, and there were many paths through the trees to other parts of the base. We walked these paths often. They were pleasant walks. However, there were loudspeakers attached to the trees that played music or made announcements. While I didn't understand most of the Russian in these announcements, they sounded like propaganda.

Just the way they juxtaposed a few measures of martial music with the announcer's emphatic voice.

The hangars were also dilapidated, and once as I approached the hanger, the loudspeakers were playing what sounded like a very old piece of Russian music on a scratchy record. Between the music and the bombed-out look of the place, I suddenly felt I had gone through a time warp and I was in the middle of a World War II scene.

Once, as we were gazing at the dilapidated structures that housed the aircraft and labs, Dryden's Center Director, Ken Szalai, was standing next to me.

"Don't tell anyone at headquarters about this place," said Ken. "They will use it as a baseline for a zero-base review of facilities."

Ken was referring to the practice at NASA for deciding the worst condition they could allow a facility to get to and then use that funding level as a baseline. The facilities here were worse than the worst they could have imagined.

## Heating Ducts

When we think of Moscow, we don't generally think of summertime. Images of fur hats and fur coats, snow, and *cold* are what we think of. While I experienced Moscow in every season and was there in every month of the year, winter is what stands out. When it is 40 degrees below zero, it is *cold.*

I carried a thermometer that only went down to -40 degrees Fahrenheit. One time the mercury dropped below that and sat in a ball at the bottom of the thermometer. What made it worse was that at Zhukovsky, the buildings had heaters, but no fuel. Heaters existed, but they couldn't afford the fuel to use in them. So we dressed as warmly as we could and huddled around the one homemade, jury-rigged space heater available in the lab.

It would have made NASA's safety folks cringe. For one of the Langley technicians, Donna Gallaher, it was too much. She insisted that we go to a hardware store and find a for-real space heater. So we did. We pooled our money and bought it for the lab.

In Moscow, most of the buildings were heated by central heating. By central heating, I mean there was a building that provided the heat for a large group of buildings around it. It was a power plant generating steam that circulated around town under the streets and sidewalks. The ducts were often man-sized.

There were several problems with this. One heat source affected a large number of buildings, offices, and apartments. If the heating plant broke down, a lot of people were without heat. It was also very inefficient because much heat would be lost in the ducts before it ever got to its intended destinations. The whole distribution system was also in disrepair.

The government decided when to turn on the heat for the season. Typically, they didn't light the fires until November — by policy — regardless of the temperature outside.

One year with a particularly cold autumn, the government made a big splash by authorizing the activation of the heat a month early — in October. This infrastructure and process was part of the residual central planning mindset of the Soviet Union.

It was not uncommon to read in the newspaper of accidents that occurred due to the heating ducts running around the city. People (and dogs) would reportedly fall into the heating ducts when sections of the sidewalk they were walking on gave way. The heat and moisture would melt the ice and snow on the sidewalks, but would also soften the earth over the ducts.

## Professor Poukhov

Professor Alexander Poukhov was the *glavne construktor* (Chief Designer) of Tupolev. He was the guiding force behind the Tu-144 program. A gregarious man of the "hail-fellow-well-met" variety, he traced his career back to working with Andrea Tupolev in designing the Tu-144 in the 1960s. He was on a mission to revive the Tu-144 and was anxious to secure our cooperation in that endeavor. Professor Poukhov was one of the few individuals I encountered at Tupolev that knew English — and would use it sometimes, even to the point of disagreeing with my use of it. (Once we had a disagreement about my use of the word *several* when he contended that I should have said *many*.) Poukhov was also a master of the toast.

The "art of toasting" figures prominently in Russian culture. With toasting comes vodka. Russian proclivity for this beverage is stereotypical. Toasting involved everyone taking shots of vodka after toasting, well, anything: Peace and brotherhood; your family; your sports team; the tie a colleague wore. The more people in the room, the more toasts. I once saw Professor Poukhov throw back 20 consecutive shots of vodka, successively toasting each person in the room individually. The professor could drink anybody under the table.

"Toast number one!" he would declare when someone gave a particularly good toast, in his estimation.

He was the diplomat, chief technical leader, cheerleader, wheeler-dealer, and spark plug for the whole operation.

## Vodka

I had heard stories of the American management teams going to Russia and getting caught up in the traditional Russian toasting ritual. Many of them woke up the following morning with massive hangovers and were unable to function in that day's meetings.

I couldn't afford that. I was not going to Russia to have ceremonial meetings. I was there to get a job done — and I was going to be there a lot. I decided that, custom or no custom, I could not set the expectation that I was going to drink. So I told the Russians up front that I don't drink — which was largely true. I didn't tell them why. They may have thought I was an alcoholic. They did think it was peculiar, but they needed me as I needed them. I provided them with equipment and they provided me with data.

So they would make jokes about it, like "You are every Russian woman's dream — a man that doesn't drink! But then they would have to ask themselves, 'Why doesn't he drink?'"

Once, the joke became a bit more edgy. "You must be a spy!" a Russian exclaimed. I laughed and raised my glass. I wasn't worried. I wasn't a spy and he knew it—I think.

He continued, "A man who doesn't drink must be a spy that needs to keep sober."

But they generally tolerated my lack of drinking. I would still toast. I put water in my glass — which looks just like vodka — and go through the ritual. I even delivered a toast in Russian once (with my interpreter translating to English). Of course, I wasn't fooling anybody. Most knew that I was substituting water for vodka — which is normally looked down upon. But, as I say, they tolerated it.

One awkward moment I experienced was during my last visit to Russia. Prof. Poukhov invited a team of us to a restaurant for dinner. This had never happened before. His wife accompanied him — also a first. We had never previously met her. She did not look happy, and at one point told her husband that he should be more like me — and not drink. So while vodka drinking is stereotypical in Russia and culturally important, it is also a huge problem. Alcoholism is rampant and during my time there I would often read in the newspaper about deaths due to consumption of "bathtub vodka." At the time it was cheaper to buy ingredients and make your own hooch in the bathtub than to buy it. Contamination added an additional risk to vodka consumption.

Once, Russians were querying me about American eating habits. One that particularly puzzled them was the "low fat" diet craze in America. I attempted to describe why Americans did that—but probably ineffectively because I, personally, wasn't convinced that a low fat diet was good for most people, especially children. One of the Russians shook his head in disbelief. "If Russians ate like that," he declared, "we would be cold, hungry, and drunk."

To further the latter point, once when I was flying to Russia I sat next to a Lithuanian woman who was employed by Westerners as a Russian interpreter. She advised me that if I wanted to avoid getting drunk, I must fill my belly with high-fat foods *before* drinking vodka. "This is what Russians do," she told me.

# Chapter 8

# Driving in and Around Moscow

## Moscow driving

There are two types of drivers in Moscow: the quick and the dead. Or, rather, the professional drivers and the amateurs who have never had a lesson. Both drive the same way: fast and aggressively. Even with my experience driving all over Europe, I had never seen anything like the driving in Moscow. I never drove there myself — nor did I want to. If the lanes were clogged, drivers would go drive in the opposite lanes — with traffic approaching — and weave through approaching cars!

There were policemen standing by the side of the road with white sticks. If they pointed the stick at you, you were to pull over. I seldom saw a seat belt that worked, but they were required. So as we approached a policeman, my driver would nudge me to lay my seatbelt across my lap — as he did. We would pass the policeman and then throw the useless seatbelts back off our laps. He wanted to give the appearance of compliance.

If there was any place I needed seatbelts, it was Moscow — and they were non-functional.

## KGB driver

The Russians' view of the driver's power was different than ours.

We would be in a meeting and a Russian would come in and tell us "The driver wants to leave!"

We'd say, "So? We're not done yet."

Our view was that we hired the driver. He took orders from us. But they treated him like the captain of a ship. He gave the orders.

One of our drivers was named Boris. He was a fiery guy who was always complaining about the other drivers — especially the amateurs. He had been a driver for the KGB and in fact was the driver that took Aleksandr Solzhenitsyn to the airport when he was expelled from the Soviet Union years before.

One day when we attended an air show at Zhukovsky, Boris was there with his daughter; and he was drunk. Fortunately, he didn't drive us that day. Later we heard that when he left the air show, his driving was so bad that even the Russians complained and the police pulled him over. He swore at them and refused to get out of his car. They broke his window, pulled him from the car, and hauled him off to jail. We never saw Boris again.

## Nineteen in a van

Russians were always looking for a ride. Many times we would find ourselves with a van full of Russians to go to town or across the airfield. We usually didn't mind this. They would find out when we were going and where, and bum a ride. I suspect this might be one reason they were sometimes insistent that because the driver wanted to go we should leave (so they could get a ride right then).

One day, after we had an exceptionally large group bumming a ride, we started telling a joke:

"How many Russians can you fit into a minivan?"

The answer is "Seventeen. You have to allow room for the two Americans."

We had 19 people in the van!

## American TV

On that occasion, I found myself with an attractive young woman sitting on my lap (which mitigated the discomfort of being packed in like sardines). She was the daughter of another woman I worked with — Marina Generalovna. Marina herself was a very attractive, pleasant woman who laughed easily with a twinkle in her eye. She was also a very skilled engineer specializing in temperature measurements and led that effort for the Russian team. She understood some English and had the respect of everyone on the project. She was always a pleasure to work with.

Marina's daughter was also an engineer. She also worked for Tupolev but I didn't know her well. Like Marina, she could speak some English, and one of the Americans asked her if she watched American TV.

"Yes. *Grace Under Fire.* It's my life," she said, pointing to herself.

That TV show was about a single working woman raising three kids. She clearly identified with that.

Some years before this, I was in Portugal for a meeting. We arranged for a tour of Lisbon one afternoon, and a bus, complete with tour guide, carted us around town. The tour guide was a young, English-speaking woman who told us that she liked American TV.

"Portuguese TV," she said, "is about rich people living in mansions. We cannot relate to that. On American programs, it is about real people. The father comes home from work, takes off his shirt, sits in front of the TV and opens a beer. A while ago I visited a friend in America at her home. Her father came home from work, took off his shirt, sat in front of the TV and opened a beer. Real life! It was exactly like on American TV!"

It is a little scary to realize that many in other countries believe that American real life is like it is on TV. I have seen the reverse play out as well. One British woman I knew was upset that a certain British TV program was popular outside Britain because it highlighted the seamier side of inner London culture.

# Chapter 9

# Money and Security

## Cash Economy

Finance in Russia worked differently than in the U.S.

Russia was pretty much a "cash and carry" economy. In fact, when they needed to fuel the aircraft, they literally brought a suitcase full of money to pay for the fuel. That cash was probably U.S. dollars, which was a very popular currency in Russia. Remember that Russian rubles were not hard currency — and were unstable. Circulation of U.S. currency in Russia was second only to its circulation in the U.S. When the $100 bill was redesigned in 1996, there was a run on the Russian banks. People wanted to trade in their old $100 bills, fearing they would now become worthless. When my Russian colleagues expressed concern about this, I tried to assure them that that's not how it worked in the U.S.

I had an experience in Spain during this period that underscores their concern. I was dining in Madrid with colleagues and one of them paid his bill with a Spanish peseta banknote that he had obtained on a previous trip. As we left the hotel, a waiter came running down the street after us, waving the banknote in an agitated manner. He spoke excitedly in Spanish and it took a while to figure out what he was so upset about. (My Spanish came in handy here.) Apparently, the banknote was too old to be considered legal tender. In the 1980s the currency had changed and the old banknotes had become obsolete. They could no longer be used to pay bills. It had never occurred to us that that might happen.

We gave him "new" money and he went away happy — and relieved.

## Pay

Things in Russia were not going well, financially. Even the people with jobs were often not being paid. One day Sasha Sudakov illustrated this for me.

Alexander (Sasha) Sudakov was my instrumentation counterpart at Tupolev. He always had a smile on his face and loved to joke. I never had any trouble working with Sash, although he spoke no English and, of course, my Russian was problematic. About the only English I ever heard Sasha speak was "Sit down, please." But electrons work the same in Russia as they do in the U.S., so in that respect we "spoke the same language," and we often found that our approach to troubleshooting a problem was the same. We had a good rapport and I enjoyed working with him.

On this day Sasha brought up the issue of their pay and he quietly motioned for me to follow him. He went to a desk drawer and pulled out a ledger showing me the accounting for their pay. He hadn't been paid for about six months! This boggles the mind of a Westerner. How do you live if you aren't being paid?

I came to understand that their housing was free (a holdover from the Soviet Union) and the economy was largely barter. Many had their own gardens where they grew their own vegetables. Many were taking second jobs as street vendors or selling wares at the flea market. Mostly this was transparent to us. But not always.

## Protest

Once we drove out to Zhukovsky with the Chief Designer, Professor Alexander Poukhov, onboard. When we arrived there, a group of women was standing near the entrance and when Poukhov got out they started speaking to him stridently. He smiled and calmed them down in a paternal manner. Eventually he got back in the van and we drove on. We had no idea what that was all about until an interpreter told us that the women were complaining about not being paid. Further, they blamed us — the Americans — for not paying them. Poukhov apparently assured them we were not to blame. (It could have been ugly.)

Now, we were paying Tupolev for the job, which we naturally assumed included paying their own people. We had no visibility into their accounting system. But it was distressing to learn that our colleagues were not being compensated — at least in a timely fashion — for the work they were doing for us. I reported this to the project leadership, but nobody seemed to know how to handle it. Russians don't take kindly to having their affairs meddled in.

## Rubles

Russia was undergoing several changes. Their currency, the ruble, was not traded on the international market and it was, in fact, not legal to take rubles out of the country. Given the fluctuations (usually downward in value) of Russian rubles, it was inadvisable to save them, anyway. For my first several trips the ruble's value was floating and getting increasingly less valuable compared to a U.S. dollar. Its value got down to about 6,000 rubles per U.S. dollar by 1998, having been about 100 rubles per dollar in 1995. In 1998 they issued the "new" ruble, which was worth 1,000 times the "old" ruble. So 6 new rubles equaled 6,000 old rubles. Both of these continued to circulate for a time, which made it rather confusing. A year after the new ruble was introduced, its value had dropped from 6 to over 20 rubles per U.S. dollar. As of this writing, the ruble exchange rate is about 58 (new) rubles per U.S. dollar. It is easy to see why U.S. dollars were the preferred currency in Russia.

## Security

One of the unsettling aspects of international travel is not really understanding what is going on around you. It is not your culture and probably not your language. You often aren't attuned to the history of the area or neighborhoods in which you find yourself. Sometimes that just means you press on in blissful ignorance of danger. The other extreme is staying holed up and not going out. What would be the point of travel?

There were bus bombings in Moscow by Chechen separatists just a few blocks from my hotel. The owner of the Radisson Hotel where I initially stayed in Moscow was gunned down in the subway entrance that I frequently used when staying there.

That said, I often felt safer travelling around European cities than American cities. I guess I understood the dangers in my own country and maybe attributed more safety than warranted in foreign cities, but the metropolitan areas in much of Europe felt more like neighborhoods with character than dangerous places. The mixture of small businesses, apartments, antique buildings, and parks — as well as the cross-section of people milling about — made me feel comfortable. I would try to dress in a manner that did not identify me as a tourist, and I tried to look deliberate about where I was going rather than standing around gawking. Chatting with someone in English could mark you as foreign, but I often wandered around by myself so there was no one to talk to anyway.

For my first several trips to Moscow, Judith would not let me wander around Moscow by myself. Judith DePaul was, among other things, the boss of the interpreters that I used. She always made sure I had a Russian interpreter with me. But a combination of saving the program money by limiting the use of interpreters on weekends — and I think more trust in my ability to navigate and stay out of trouble — meant that on later trips I did a lot of solo excursions around town.

# Chapter 10

# Managing the Program

## Program management

While the American "side" was paying for the flights, Tupolev still absorbed some of the cost of resurrecting the airplane. American managers are used to having significant insight into the progress of the projects they manage. The Tupolev model for American managerial involvement was 1) insert money here and 2) get flight data there. They would insist that everything was on schedule — long after it became apparent (at least to me) that the flight was going to slip. But you couldn't get them to say that until just days before the flight. This made planning hard, and frustrated the managers in the U.S. Once, in an attempt to get more insight into the Russian process for flight safety, the American managers asked me to look into how the Tupolev process worked. I asked Edgar Krupyanski, the Tupolev chief of the flight team (or chief engineer) how their process of determining flight readiness worked. From the questions I was asking, it was obvious I was clueless how they did things.

Krupyanski remarked "I am surprised that you don't know the process."

Another Russian reminded him that it would be hard for me to know since I wasn't invited to the meetings. He grunted, and then begrudgingly tried to describe the process to me.

The reality was that when Tupolev held a flight readiness review, it was a "dog and pony show." Everyone would gather around the table and respond with an affirmative when asked if their areas were ready for flight. They always were. This meeting was not held until problems had been worked out. It was a formality. Any working meeting they may have had to discuss issues we were never allowed to observe.

## Teleconferences

Communication between the States and Russia was difficult, relying largely on faxes and travel. This was long before Webexes, Zoom calls, and even reliable email. Given the lack of a common workday between the two countries, telephoning was a fairly rare event — but sometimes had to be attempted. I say "attempted" because calls seldom went smoothly. The telephone infrastructure in Russia was poor; even phoning between Moscow and Zhukovsky, a distance of 30 miles, was difficult, as I mentioned before. Trying to carry on a telephone conversation between Russia and the United States was tempting fate. It often took 15 minutes to establish contact and make sure we knew who all was on the line and could hear each other (the lines were often static-ridden). Then there was another five or ten minutes to get the pleasantries attended to — and interpreted. Then after 30 minutes, like clockwork, we would lose the connection and have to start the process over. So we might get ten minutes of productive discussion in a one-hour teleconference.

## Abbey Express

For a year or so I had another option for flying to Moscow. NASA was gearing up for Russian collaboration on the new space station, and The Johnson Space Center Director, George Abbey, contracted for a charter service to fly regular flights to Moscow. These flights were dubbed the "Abbey Express." The flights originated in Houston, made a stop or two at other NASA centers on the way to Washington, D.C., and then flew on to Moscow by way of Gander, Newfoundland, and Keflavik,

Iceland. So I would fly commercial to D.C., wait about six hours for the charter to show up, then join up with it. Despite the layover, I liked the flight because it was uncrowded, took me to out-of-the-way places on the way to Moscow, then took us into a very un-busy airport, Vnukovo, where they would often open up the passport control booths just for us; so there was no waiting for hours hemmed in by fellow humanity like I often experienced at Sheremetyevo Airport. Then a chartered bus would whisk us directly to our hotel. It was much less stressful travel.

On one such flight, however, one of the flight attendants got real chummy with a group of the passengers and they partied all night — when I was trying to sleep. I was told later she didn't have an entry visa into Russia and the airline was fined; and she was fired. I don't know if it was true, but seemed like karma to me.

The Abbey Express flights were ended for financial reasons. I was on a number of flights where there were only about six passengers. Great for me. Bad for the agency.

## Russ Barber

During one meeting in Moscow, Russ Barber, who was the Dryden project manager tracking the flight project, leaned over to Professor Poukhov.

"Professor Poukhov," he said, "I want to ask you a very important question … Do you think OJ Simpson is guilty?"

I was amused because I was pretty sure that Poukhov didn't even know who Simpson was. I suspect the weight Russ gave to the subject was due to a little too much vodka.

Russ was a good project manager. I had known him for years, and worked on other projects he managed. One in particular, the KC-135 Winglet flight project, really established my reputation for designing flight instrumentation systems. I came to Russ and asked him if I could fly a system I was developing onboard his aircraft. There was plenty of room for my hardware (it was a tanker). He agreed, as long as the system could be easily reconfigured to bypass my system should it have problems. That was fair. What my system did was allow data to be examined in real time during a flight — onboard the aircraft.

It worked. Then serendipity came into play. The flight plan for the Winglet flight project called for flying six or seven hours *outside* of the Dryden telemetry coverage area, or range, so our control room could not direct the flight based on real-time data from the aircraft. However, my system would allow the test lead engineer to fly *onboard* the aircraft and direct from there regardless of where the plane was.

So now my system went from being an "OK to fly if it doesn't interfere" to a "must have — won't fly without it." Russ remembered that 15 years later and put a lot of faith in my work, which made my job working on the Tu-144LL easier.

**Fred**

We called him "Fred." Fred was not a Russian, nor was he exactly American. But he was a member of the Tu-144LL project team, even though he wasn't alive. Fred was a picture. He was an idea conjured up by Russ Barber, who felt that presenting him as a gift to Professor Poukhov would be a good idea.

The picture he envisioned was a large photograph of the Tu-144, mounted in a wooden frame and backlit by a fluorescent light. When Russ first proposed it, I was not sanguine about it; I saw too many logistical problems. But Russ was paid to think of ways to make the project go, and I was paid to find ways of making his visions work.

Normally dealing with something like this would not be a big problem. Our shops and photo lab could manufacture it; but there were complications.

First, the power source in Russia is different than in the U.S. They use 220 volt AC, 50 Hz power and we use 110 volt AC, 60 Hz power. This means that the ballast of the light would have to be changed to something not commonly available in the States. OK. Do-able. Second, Fred would have to be transported to Russia — and Russ decided that he should be hand-carried.

Now, I hand-carried a lot of things to Russia during the program. My checked bags were usually maxed out, which in those days meant two bags at 75 pounds apiece. I had test equipment and other hardware, as well as documentation (paper is heavy) and often a lot of cold-weather gear. But Fred represented another level of problem. He was too big for a carry-on and too fragile to check as baggage; so he was packaged in a (heavy) wooden frame.

Russ had Fred delivered to my house and he drove his pickup truck over the next day to take it to the airport. We hoisted him in the back and started to lash it into the truck.

"You're the Eagle Scout," Russ said to me. "Why don't you lash it down?"

I struggled a bit to figure out the best knots to use, and ultimately Russ, who was growing increasingly impatient, said "Why don't you use a "trucker's hitch?""

There was a very good reason I didn't use a trucker's hitch; I didn't know how to tie one. (It was not on the Boy Scout knot syllabus.)

"Here, let me do it," he said. In short shrift he had Fred all lashed down and ready to start his adventure. We drove to the airport, 75 miles away, and "checked" him in. It was obviously over the size and weight limits for normal baggage.

At this point you might think we were done with the hard part, but there was another wrinkle. Our flight was to Washington, D.C., where we were to transfer to the "Abbey Express" flight to Moscow. Since this was a charter flight that took off from a different part of the airport, we had to retrieve it from baggage claim and manhandle it over to the charter area. Then we started scratching our heads over how to get Fred on board the (rather small) jet. It turned out that the luggage area wasn't large enough for him and he was too big to take on board.

But since it *was* a charter flight we had some latitude. We decided to uncrate Fred and carry the now unprotected picture on board, where we then wedged him between two rows of seats. The "Abbey" flights were usually pretty lightly populated so it didn't deprive anyone of a seat. We flew on to Moscow.

Arriving at Vnukovo Airport, we got Fred through customs and manhandled him into the bus for transport to the hotel; where I stowed him in my room.

Fred's fame had spread, and NASA Associate Administrator Rich Christianson, who was in Moscow representing the NASA Administrator, wanted to see it. So he came to my room and sat on my bed to admire it. This, I thought, was not a very dignified manner in which to meet him for the first time. But Rich, an impressively large man, never let dignity stand in the way of getting things done.

Fred's journey was not quite over, however. We still had to get him to the Boeing facility in downtown Moscow. We now had access to our own ground transportation, so that was accomplished without much difficulty. The picture was presented the next day amidst great fanfare.

I could never look at that picture — or think of Russ — without the saga of "Fred" coming to mind.

# Chapter 11

# Languages

## Paris

Before I ever set foot in Russia and after Russians had visited us a few times in the States, I was sent to France to be trained in the instrumentation data acquisition system the Russians would be using on the Tu-144. Tupolev had arranged to buy a French system — the Damien V — and the training class would be in Massy Palaiseau, which was a short distance south of Paris. So I stayed in a small hotel in Paris near the Jardin du Luxembourg and every day for two weeks took the train south to Massy Palaiseau. (I got very good at asking for a round trip ticket in French — *Un billet pour Massy Palaiseau. Aller-retour.* Well, it was good enough to get me the tickets.)

The course was taught by a Frenchman speaking English and then interpreted into Russian for the benefit of the Russian team that would be installing and using the system. I was there so that I would understand it too, since I needed to interface to it via the Russian team. Sometimes, when I would ask a question in English the Frenchman could not understand me. Comically, our Russian interpreter, Sergei, would repeat my question *in English* and the Frenchman would understand *him*. Sergei said he should be paid more for this extra interpretation.

Everybody associates the term *Bistro* with a small French restaurant. I discovered that its origin is actually Russian. The story is that when Napoleon straggled back to France after disastrously occupying Moscow, his troops were tailed by Russians — who then entered Paris. They would sit in the French eating establishments and pound the table, shouting *"Bistro! Bistro!"* to encourage faster service. *Bistro* in Russian means "quickly."

The name stuck.

In a turn-about, the subways in Moscow were built by the French, and a token used to get through the turnstiles was called a *jeton* by the Russians — which is the French word for "token."

Travelling around Paris during our time off was made more interesting by doing it with the Russian team. This touring was useful as an icebreaker with the Russians and I got a perspective that was enhanced by two sets of foreigners from different countries touring a third country. Once, one of the Russians, a programmer, was upset because he saw a small yard — not more than maybe 15 feet by 15 feet — that was a lawn planted with grass.

"They should be planting vegetables there!" he exclaimed. "What are they going to eat in the winter?"

He had never been out of Russia before. Many Western practices befuddled him. He often didn't like what he saw and was vocal about it. It was an interesting perspective.

One evening a few of us were invited to share dinner with Judith DePaul. She had made reservations at a restaurant that was rather expensive. (Judith never did anything cheaply.) We had a private, enclosed, booth.

The food was good. The conversation was lively, and we were told that the booth we were in used to be routinely reserved by Francois Mitterrand — the former president of France — for his romantic "assignations."

## Not Deaf

Being in meetings where the participants did not speak the same language often had interesting dynamics. Everything went through the interpreter — a Russian who didn't work for the Russian Tupolev company and was hired by the Americans. That arrangement worked well because each side felt some claim to his loyalty. However, there was always the desire to talk directly to our counterparts on the other "side." By the way, the use of the term "U.S. side" or "Russian side" always bothered me. To me it promoted the idea that we were on *different* sides, not all pulling for the same goal. I avoided its use where I could. I would refer to the "American *team*" or the "Russian *team*" — which felt more inclusive to me.

One time, Sasha Sudakov was talking to me in Russian and his voice was getting progressively louder with each exchange. The interpreter was doing his job, but at one point Mr. Sablev — a Russian manager that seemed to be ubiquitous — stopped Sasha in the middle of a sentence and made a calming gesture to him as he spoke.

The interpreter told me he said, "Sash, Sash. Tone it down. He's not deaf, just foreign." That brought a laugh from all, and Sasha continued in a more subdued voice.

It was comforting to me to see that wasn't just an American mistake. There seems to be a universal expectation that if you just speak loudly enough, a foreigner must surely understand you even if he doesn't speak the language.

## Cognates

One of my interpreters, Michael Melnichenko, had a seven-year-old son. One day, he asked his father to teach him

English. So Michael started with some cognates (words that are the same in both languages).

"How do you say 'sport' in English?" he asked his son in Russian.

"I don't know," his son replied.

"Sport," Michael supplied.

"How do you say 'computer' in English?"

"Computer?" answered his son, tentatively.

"Yes. How do you say 'football'?"

"Football," came his son's more confident answer. "Well," his son exclaimed, "what's the use in learning English? All the words are the same as Russian."

Many words *are* the same, although you couldn't tell it by looking at the words on paper — because the alphabets are different. I would have to sound out a Russian word, only to sometimes discover that it was, in fact, an English word just transliterated into Russian.

## Driver's daughter

One of my drivers had a 15-year-old daughter whom he often brought with him when he drove me to the airport to return home. She was studying English and I represented an opportunity to practice with a native speaker. She was bright and engaging and had a pretty good command of the language. I am always impressed when I hear mastery of English by a foreigner. It was a pleasure to talk with her.

## My Russian

The interpreters I had available to me were excellent. We contracted with IBP to provide them, as well as a driver. The interpreters were highly skilled technical interpreters. We were dealing with a highly technical project full of aerospace and electronic jargon and my interaction with the Russians was largely seamless, although delayed by having to filter everything through the interpreter each way. Our interpreters were all Russians and we got along well with all of them. Every once in a while, though, they made a mistake. It was rare, but one incident sticks in my mind.

At the end of each visit I would write a "summary of discussions" that summarized the activities of the visit, what decisions were made, what requests were made, and what equipment was transferred. We came to realize, after a few visits, that these documents were more than just a trip report. To the Russian team, they represented marching orders. They prioritized what we expected them to do next. In essence, they had the force of a contract.

In this instance I was going over the equipment list a few items at a time and waiting for the interpreter to translate what I said into Russian, when I noticed puzzled expressions on the faces of the Russian team. So I repeated what I said and this time cocked an ear to what the interpreter was saying — in Russian. I could tell he was saying it wrong. So in desperation I repeated what I had said — in Russian this time. They looked startled, and from that point on they were never really sure just how much Russian I knew. Some would walk up to me and start chattering away in Russian, assuming I knew what they were saying (not often the case). Others would go off into a corner and whisper so that I would not overhear their Russian conversations.

**Rizzi Russian**

Steve Rizzi was the NASA Langley Research Center lead experimenter for the cabin noise experiment, which studied noise levels inside the aircraft cabin. He and his team were often in Russia to facilitate the installation of his experiment on the Tu-144LL. Steve had learned some Russian before coming to Russia. His wife had studied it in college and he had worked with her to pick up some Russian. My knowledge of Russian was, in principle, greater than his, but he was not reticent to engage Russians with the Russian that he knew. He put me to shame. I was much more timid and afraid to put myself "out there" by exposing my limitations. Steve, however, by his example encouraged me to come more out of my shell and make the attempt. Once, the Russian woman who filed for my entry visas, Olga, asked me — in somewhat halting English — if I spoke Russian.

I rattled off a phrase in Russian that I had memorized that translated: "I speak Russian very poorly. I know few words."

Olga's eyes widened in surprise and she replied, "Oh, you speak it very well!"

The problem with rattling off phrases with a credible accent is that people then assume you know the language much better than you actually do. However, that can stretch you and improve your language skills if you are open to making yourself more vulnerable. People really do appreciate the effort. What made my experience in Russia unique is that I understood Russian better than my Russian colleagues understood English. Without the interpreter, that made the default language Russian. In all other countries I had visited, when the going got tough, English was the go-to because their knowledge of English exceeded my knowledge of the local language.

## Obscenities

I had run across a book in the States that was a dictionary of Russian obscenities. Intrigued, I bought it. Every day, when in Russia, a van would pick me up and drive me out to Zhukovsky

65

airbase — about 30 miles out of Moscow. One day, the American team from NASA Langley was driving with me and I showed the dictionary to Steve Rizzi. He delightedly started reading Russian obscenities out loud, much to the amusement of our Russian driver. Steve, in fact, found occasions in more formal settings to try out his new-found skill, with mixed results. He swore at Mr. Sablev, a manager well known to us by this point of the program, and nearly got called out to duel. He used the same expression with Professor Poukhov, who was enchanted. Steve became his best friend.

One of my interpreters was very interested in this dictionary and persuaded me to loan it to him as I left Russia following one of my visits. The next time I returned he was sporting a black eye and some cuts on his face. I asked about his injuries and he reluctantly told me that he had been mugged and his briefcase was stolen. Further, my dictionary was in his briefcase. He was upset about that and took pains to find a replacement for it. What he found was a dictionary of obscenities that was published in Russia. I found this one even more interesting than mine because they would take Russian expressions and translate them *literally* into English — often with hilarious results.

I still have that dictionary and refer to it on occasion when I need a laugh.

## Foreign Languages

One phenomena I have noticed (and maybe it's just how my brain works) is that I seem to know two languages — English and "foreign." When I am struggling to come up with a word in Russian, or Spanish, or German, my mind often doesn't differentiate between them. For example, if I am trying to come up with the phrase "I'm ready" in Russian, my mind first goes to *estoy listo* (Spanish). If I want to say "let's go" in German, I am thinking "лошли (*poshli*)," which is Russian.

I am reminded of a family story about my great-great grandfather, who had ten children. When he was disciplining one, he sometimes had to run through the names from oldest to youngest until he got to the right one.

"Stella! Otis! Ezra! Lula! Orin! Ah, Orin! Stop that!"

# Chapter 12

# The Job

## On-site Engineer

My job on the Tu-144LL project was to facilitate acquiring and installing the instrumentation system and sensors for all the experiments (there were six); establish the means of transferring calibrated flight data to the U.S.; and to facilitate answering any questions between the Russian team and American team. I was, in essence, the U.S. representative in Russia — the liaison or so-called "on-site engineer." While I wasn't in project management, and I was not working for Boeing (which had that responsibility as the prime contractor) I was the guy there. I was often the only American on site at the Tupolev facilities in Russia. That made me the principal point of contact — the face of the American team. Remember that the Internet was still young. Email access for the Russian team was practically non-existent. The Russian phone system was poor, and the time difference was 11 hours between Moscow and the West Coast of the United States, where my home base was.

## Boeing

As part of this job, I made many on-the-spot decisions about the conduct of the program. Many of them, in my opinion, were unquestionably appropriate for me to make in my role as instrumentation engineer — such as designing the form for passing flight data and metadata back to the U.S. This torqued off some in Boeing management, because as the prime contractor they felt they should be making those decisions.

In the abstract they were probably correct for some things that I ruled on, but in practical terms the distance, time-zone separation, translation, and communication barriers would have brought the project to a standstill without on-the-spot decisions. You needed to be *boots on the ground* for progress to be made. This came to a head during one teleconference I had with the American team while I was in Moscow. I advised Norm Princen — the handling qualities researcher from Douglas Aircraft cum Boeing team — that if he wanted to coordinate flight planning for the next flight, now was a good time to come to Moscow. This seemingly innocuous piece of advice exacted an angry reaction from Pradeep Parikh, the Boeing deputy program manager.

"I don't know how they do things at NASA," he declared with feeling, "but at Boeing we let our *managers* make those decisions!"

After a stunned silence, I responded, "Well, I don't know how they do things at Boeing, but at NASA we like to give managers information on which they can *base* their decisions."

His boss, the Boeing program manager, Dan Smith, at another time had directed me to send all of my faxes to Russia through his office. I allowed as how my faxes were an extension of the work I did on site in Russia and if he really wanted to slow down the project, then requiring his approval for all my communications when I was off-site would certainly do it. I suggested to Boeing that if they really wanted to make project decisions, they needed to be *on site*. While they did have a proxy on site in the form of a Russian they hired, this was not the same to Tupolev as having an American there.

I offered to copy Dan on all of my correspondence, which he reluctantly agreed to and I subsequently did. After the flight program wound up, successfully, Dan confided to me that despite his misgivings, the system I came up with for getting the job done had worked.

## Holding Court

As I said, if you weren't there in Russia and questions arose, it could cause significant delays; so I made the communication happen. Often, I would sit in a conference room and "hold court." One Russian after another would enter the room and make their request for equipment or information. I would write it down and either answer or relay back to the States that evening via email. I felt like the "godfather." *What can I do for you?*

By the same token, if someone on the American team had a question, I would ask my Russian program contacts and they would let me talk to the appropriate person to answer it. For example, our Rockwell contractor, Warren Beaulieu, had a question about the fuel system, so Tupolev sent in the man who *designed* the fuel system for the Tu-144. He sketched out the system on a piece of paper while I scribbled copious notes, apologizing for the fact that my knowledge of fuel systems was minimal. He was gracious and patiently explained many things that would have been unnecessary were I a fuel systems expert. Then that evening I relayed the information back to the U.S.

These interactions were complicated by the language barrier. None of the Russians I worked with daily spoke English. Those who knew English had left the program early on because English-speaking was an asset in Moscow and they could get actual *paying* jobs using that skill. (For example, Lyudmila — a Tupolev programmer who was attractive and spoke English — got a job selling perfume at a store.) So I found myself in the peculiar position of knowing more Russian than my counterparts knew English. The forced me on several occasions to use Russian when my interpreter was out of earshot.

## Windows Surprises

In the mid-1990s, the Microsoft operating system in common use was Windows 3.1. Tupolev was using a Russian version. Sometimes I had to use their machines and navigating around the windows was problematic. I had to either translate the Russian or recognize the position of a command in a drop-down list. One day, I was asked to help them with a problem. It seemed that a file copy operation was not working and they asked me to take a look at it. While the file was copying, a little animation appeared to pass the time. It was a file folder flying across from one file to another, along with a count-down timer estimating time to completion of transfer. When the counter got to zero the folder continued to fly.

"See," they said, "it didn't work."

"Wait for it," I said.

Sure enough, after about 30 more seconds the transfer completed. I explained to them that the transfer time estimate was sometimes way off. One of them shook his head slowly and exclaimed, in heavily accented English, "It surprising Bill Gates still alive."

## Viruses

Computer viruses were a problem. This was a time before our systems had routine virus sweeps and proactive file scanning when copying files into our machine. I routinely received files from the Russians (mostly data) and loaded them onto my laptop. At one point I noticed that the plotting program I had written in Matlab language script was not working as expected, which I managed to work around. When I returned home I obtained some virus scanning software and found an enormous amount of corrupted files on my laptop computer.

71

After repairing the damage, my Matlab plotting program started working again; and I became much more proactive in checking media that I attached to my computer.

# Chapter 13

# The Aircraft

## Cockpit

Russian designs are typically functional and boxy. The Tu-144 cockpit was no exception. It was not streamlined and to me it resembled the engineering flight simulators we would build up at Dryden. The coloration was interesting, too. It was a kind of bluish-green that I learned was popular in Russian military cockpits.

## Flight Recorder Temperature

Working in the airplane was not a lot of fun when it was cold. It's hard to press buttons with gloves on, so you'd have to take them off. It was so cold that some of our equipment wouldn't run. We had to heat up the cabin first. For our flight recorder, that became a problem, and I consulted the manufacturer. They said there were a few resistors that controlled the temperature cutoff and they could be changed, but they normally do that at the factory. As the unit was in Russia, the customs paperwork associated with extracting the unit, sending it to the factory, modifying it, and sending it back to Russia was daunting — and time-consuming. So they agreed to send a technician out to Dryden in California and train *me* how to do it. Then I went to Russia and modified the unit myself on site. Pretty scary: an engineer with a soldering iron.

## CoCom Limits

Export control was another issue.

In those days Dryden didn't export out of the country very much, and the procedures to do that were being written at NASA headquarters. I would call the export control officer at headquarters and say, "This is what I need to do and how I plan to do it" and they would say "Sounds OK" — and then write a procedure for it. Sometimes I'd have to export from the U.S. to Russia. Sometimes it was from France to Russia. The Russians were very diligent about keeping track of our equipment and returning it at the end of the program. A few items did go missing, however — including a data recorder worth more than $100,000.

One piece of equipment that was particularly difficult to export was the Global Positioning System (GPS) units to be used on the Tu-144. GPS units standardly have altitude and speed limits imposed on them. If you were to travel over 1200 miles per hour ground speed or exceed 59,000 feet in altitude, the unit is supposed to shut off its data transmission (to prevent use on intercontinental ballistic missile-type applications). These are called "CoCom" limits after an abbreviation of the name "Coordinating Committee for Multilateral Export Controls" — the name of the committee that established the limits. Since the Tu-144 was to exceed both of those limitations, we sought to get the limits removed. Major problem. Normally these limits are only removed for U.S. military purposes. They allowed NASA to remove them too, but this unit was to be exported — and exported to *Russia*. Red flags all over the place (so to speak). We let Boeing handle the paperwork, and were happy to do so. It took many months and 17 signatures — including the assistant secretary of state — to get it authorized.

So we were set. The unit was installed on the aircraft and performed to expectations.

However, there was a time limit on the license — which expired before the end of the program, which had been extended. So we sought to renew the license, and hit roadblocks everywhere. First off, the Russian security service had re-asserted itself and insisted that regardless of what we did next, we had to "un-export" the unit back to the United States when the export license expired. Then Boeing decided they wanted no part of going through the hassle of getting a new export license with the co-com limits removed. They had just run afoul of U.S. export regulations and were levied a $10 million fine to settle allegations that they had violated export control laws in their project to launch satellites from a converted oil rig platform. They were smarting from that and wanted nothing to do with another export issue they could avoid.

"You guys do it — U.S. government to U.S. government," they told us.

We also were short on time. It would probably take longer to get it approved than we had time left on the program. So we punted. We sent the Russian unit back to the U.S. and then exported a standard unit to Russia — a much quicker process. We installed that unit on the Tu-144LL and resigned ourselves to losing data at high altitude and ground speed. It was most critical at landing anyway.

We flew and then analyzed the data. To my surprise we didn't lose any of the high altitude or high speed data! I then realized that the limitations only applied to data *transmitted* in real time, NOT to raw data recorded on board. This made sense, as the sensitivity was to units being part of a guidance, navigation, and control (GNC) system — which would need real-time (transmitted) data. The raw files were just that — raw — and not in a form usable by a GNC system. The raw data was just recorded. While the recording could be pulled later and translated into navigational data, it would be too late to affect the trajectory of a missile. We had gone through all the pain and suffering of State Department approval for nothing.

## Calibration Lab

One day I was given a tour of the pressure sensor calibration lab at Zhukovsky. Mr. Sperny, who headed the lab, was conducting it. They demonstrated the calibration process and then Mr. Sperny turned to me and said (through the interpreter) "So tell me, are we behind?"

Another awkward moment for me because, well, yes, they were. The equipment and procedure they used were antiquated when I started as a young engineer more than 20 years before. As it happened, my first assignment as an engineering student at NASA was to automate the pressure transducer calibration process — which I did in the early 1970s. So I was familiar with the process and knew what I was looking at.

However, not wanting to embarrass anyone with an impolitic answer, I responded, "Well, at NASA we have automated the process, but I have discovered that in so doing the technicians have lost touch with the physics of the situation."

The technician who was conducting the test pulled herself up to her full height and proclaimed, "I understand the physics of the situation."

I indicated my approval and we moved on.

Leaving someone with their pride is always a good idea.

## Power/resources

I used a workbench in the instrumentation lab at Zhukovsky to check out my equipment. I was having difficulty with a decommutator (a unit that cracks data out of a telemetry stream), which was acting flaky. One day, as I touched the bench with my wrists while also touching the unit, I received a shock — so I measured the voltage difference between the metal bench and the power ground; it was 90 volts! That's a lot. Not very safe.

Unreliability of power was expected even in the instrumentation systems at Tupolev. Even the instrumentation system calibration process assumes that the voltage feeding the transducers will fluctuate. They do a "ratiometric" calibration in which for each measurement you measure the voltage powering the sensor and compute the ratio between them. It helps compensate for irregularities in the power.

Russians are very resourceful. I carried an inkjet printer with me to allow me to do make hardcopies on the go. It didn't have a lot of capacity, but it worked for one or two sheets at a time. One day I blithely plugged it into my power plug adapter and then plugged that into the wall. *Pop!* The power light was not on. I sniffed it; it was smoked. I realized instantly what had happened. I had fried the power converter because I had plugged it into the wrong voltage. I knew better than that. European wall sockets are twice the voltage of U.S. wall sockets. Normally I buy units that will accept either voltage but had gotten sloppy and didn't check that for the printer power converter. It was a 110 volt-only device, and I had just plugged it into the 220 volt outlet. Not good.

The next day I embarrassingly admitted to the Russians what I had done and they offered to take a look at it and see what they could do. The next day they returned it to me — functional. They had repaired the unit and also hay-wired a transformer to convert 220 volts to 110 volts — which they presented to me. I used that transformer for the rest of the program. It was heavy. It wasn't pretty. But it worked.

This was an excellent demonstration of Russian ingenuity and resourcefulness. They take the material they have on hand

and use it to get the job done. It often isn't pretty, but it works —and usually works reliably. They have to make tradeoffs. "Fly the plane versus fix the toilet" kind of tradeoffs. They often couldn't obtain new resources; they had to make do with what was lying around. There was no "Amazon" to call and no money with which to buy new things — and until recently no access to the materials anyway.

One of my language instructors at DLI was a Russian engineer who used to work in a Soviet factory. If something broke and it needed replacement, he would spend days running around town looking for a replacement. When he immigrated to the United States, he got a job as a maintenance man at a factory — a job considerably below his education. When something broke there, he hesitantly approached his boss with the bad news. His boss reached over, picked up the phone, called a supplier, cradled the phone and said, "It will be here tomorrow." He was amazed! This illustrated for him the stark contrast between the Soviet Union and the United States when it came to product availability and service.

Shopping for Russians in Soviet times was a problem. Stores weren't stocked and sales people weren't motivated to help customers. More work for them and no reward for more work. The supply chain was often broken. Production decisions were made that were decoupled from demand. Russians got used to standing in line for products. I was told that if they saw a line they would go stand in it — and *then* find out what the line was for. If people were waiting for it, it must be desirable to have.

Now in the post-Soviet era and working with Americans, Russians had a glimpse of what was possible — and it was magic to them. When the Russian group of managers first came to the United States and visited NASA Langley in Hampton Roads, Virginia, the first thing they wanted to do was to go to a Walmart and shop. They walked in and saw a massive store *filled* with products and their eyes got big. They ran around pulling blue jeans and shoes off the shelves and brought them up for purchase. "You can try them on in fitting rooms over there," I told them. They shook their heads.

"No need," they said. "The size doesn't matter." They intended to provide them to family and friends — and sell some. This kind of product just wasn't available in Moscow.

# Chapter 14

# Socializing

## Mark Twain

One day we were sitting around, chatting. I don't remember how the subject came up, but Sasha Sudakov mentioned that Mark Twain (Samuel Clemens) was a very popular author in Russia. In fact, his wife, as a prize for an academic achievement in school, had been given a copy of one of his books — in Russian.

"You know," I said casually, "Mark Twain is a relative of mine."

They got very excited.

"Really!?" Sasha said in Russian, and talked animatedly with the other Russians. "How is he related?"

"He is my great-great grandfather's second cousin," I told them — which was true. My great-great grandfather's brother had written a family genealogy in the 1930s tracing the Clemens roots back to the early 17th century. I also had seen a genealogy researched independently by a professional genealogist that confirmed it. While this was a source of great pride in our family, some — like my 102-year-old great-great aunt Lyde — were not enamored with his irreverence. She would scowl when his name was brought up.

The next day, Sasha handed me the book *Tom Sawyer* written in Russian.

"It is my wife's book," he declared. "Will you sign it?"

"Uh, but he's a *distant* relative," I said.

"Well, don't put in *that* part," he said.

So I somewhat amusedly took the book and inscribed inside the front cover:

"From the banks of the Mississippi River to the banks of the Moscow River, I send you greetings."

I signed it "Glenn Bever, relative of Mark Twain."

Sasha was happy. He had a book autographed by a relative of one of Russia's most beloved authors.

I guess all that toasting paid off when called upon to write something appropriate in an autograph.

## Education

Many subjects would come up as we relaxed around food. Over lunch one day at Tupolev in Moscow we fell into a discussion about the sounds animals make — as depicted in Russian and English. For example, ducks go *krya-krya* in Russia instead of *quack-quack* like they do in America. Dogs go *gahf-gahf*. Pigs go *khryoo-khryoo*. Sometimes the sounds are cognates. Cats go *meow* in America and *myaoo* in Russia. You can see that not all our discussions were serious.

Another time we fell to talking about educational systems both in Russian and America. They described a system where students would take tests and their aptitude would determine the profession they would go into. Student preference was not a factor. The education itself was "free." I described a system in the U.S. where students would take tests to determine aptitude and performance, but they would also decide what field they wanted to pursue. Their testing would inform their decision. They would then have to apply to schools and be accepted — and then usually pay for the education.

One of the Russians declared that the American system was better. The freedom of choice appealed to him. Their system was another example of centralized planning versus individual choice that was prevalent in their culture, but Western ideas were beginning to have an impact.

On the other hand, one of my interpreters once told me that "Under communism, we were encouraged to do our best. Under capitalism, we are encouraged to do our worst."

I believe what he saw was idealism versus practicality. Communism — particularly the version operating in Russia — for all of its ills, was a known quantity and people knew how to navigate it. People weren't under the illusion that the government was telling them the truth, but the lip service was duty to the mother country and the collective good.

Now, Russia was undergoing a massive change in mindset, and things were rather chaotic. New rules were being applied. Nobody was applying the "common good" standard, but rather the "individual good" standard. Since looking out for yourself was officially panned under the communist regime, the new system would be regarded as "doing your worst" by those used to hearing the old rhetoric.

When I was at the Defense Language Institute, one of my Russian instructors complained that in America she didn't know how to "expedite" things. In Russia, she knew who to bribe. In America, you couldn't bribe officials to get things done more quickly. An interesting perspective. Fairness can get in the way of the individual with an agenda. What we would regard as "doing your best" by an official she regarded as an impediment to getting her job done.

I guess fairness is in the eye of the beholder.

## Bush's Legs

During the transition from the Soviet Union to the Russian Federation, the United States sought to help things along. Apparently, President George H.W. Bush arranged for shipments of chicken to be sent to Russia. The chickens were not whole chickens. They were only chicken legs. A *lot* of chicken legs. The Russians thought this was peculiar. *Where are the rest of the chickens?* they wanted to know. Chicken legs became synonymous with a new name they gave them: "Bush's legs." And they'd laugh whenever they said it.

Another type of legs are worth noting — those of Russian women. Not being dead and having eyes, I noticed that the young Russian women strolling around Moscow had outstandingly shapely legs. I suspect it comes from all the walking they do. Sergei Karabonov, my interpreter, commented that there is an old proverb to the effect that Slavic women, while very beautiful in their youth, "turn into babushkas (grandmothers) when they get older."

## Saunas

Russians love saunas. I grew up in the American Midwest near the confluence of the Missouri and Mississippi Rivers, and the concept of adding humidity to hot air didn't appeal to me. Memories of the hot, sticky days of summer help me appreciate the dryness of the desert where I now live.

I wasn't pressured to do saunas in Russia, but having expressed my displeasure at the concept, I cut off a potential way of bonding.

"You would get more invitations if you liked saunas," they told me.

Early in the program, I was taken out to the forest in Russia for a picnic. We roamed the fields and Tatyana, a Russian project manager, picked flowers. She made them into a wreath and placed it on my head. It was a day of simple friendship. Mr. Sablev was running the expedition, and he brought his 14-year-old daughter with him.

Mr. Sablev always seemed to be in charge. He was a pleasant man who always maintained a certain dignity. He was often present in our meetings and social functions. While most of the Russians we ended up calling by their first names, we never called him by his, which was Vyatcheslav, or Slava. We always called him "Mr. Sablev."

We made several excursions early in the program with our Russian hosts. We visited the Bolshoi Ballet, toured Moscow visiting museums, and attended a Russian circus performance. While the Bolshoi is well known to the West, the circus was very much a performance by and for a Russian audience. These excursions served to provide an informal mechanism for us getting to know each other better — and gave us a better acquaintance with the culture we were trying to work with.

# Chapter 15

# International Relations

## NATO

I had some interesting discussions with the Russians relating to the North Atlantic Treaty Organization (NATO). Historically, NATO was formed to counter the Soviet threat to Europe. Russia had gobbled up Eastern Europe as a "buffer." Having been invaded more than once, most recently by NAZI Germany, they are sensitive to the potential for it happening again. The Soviet Union is no more, but the history remains fresh in their mind — perhaps even enhanced, given their weakened state. On the other hand, the recently liberated Eastern European countries were anxious to join NATO as a buffer against another invasion *by Russia*. Of course, that eventuality eats into the Russian buffer so they were not anxious to see the NATO alliance expanded.

Russians that I talked to could not understand why the West would stir up problems by entertaining a NATO expansion. Most Westerners could not understand why Russia would be so opposed to it now that Russia and we were friends. I think many of the former Eastern Bloc countries regarded the NATO membership to be a precursor to European Union membership and an economic alliance. The United States would not be sanguine about Russia forming military alliances with, say, Mexico or Canada, and would wonder about their motivation for doing so. No surprise that the Russians had concerns, too.

I was in an awkward spot. One of my other NASA duties was serving on a NATO group dealing with flight test. So I was kind of in the middle. Generally I tried to avoid political discussions but the NATO topic was something on the Russians' minds and the subject would come up from time to time. I tried to assure them that Americans had no ulterior motives in entertaining these new alliances. I did, however, agree that such actions could be seen as provocative.

Similarly, once when I was eating in a restaurant in England with my NATO team, our waitress decided to engage us in a political discussion. She seemed to hold us personally responsible for the actions of our president, who at the time was George W. Bush. I should say that she was equally incensed at her own prime minister, Tony Blair, who was acting in concert with President Bush. Now, none of us were anxious to get into it, and as I looked around the table I realized that I didn't know the political leanings of my colleagues. As government employees we were well practiced at avoiding such discussions with other government employees. We were strictly non-partisan while working. In this situation, we weren't technically working, but any political discussion could have ramifications to relationships when we were. Further, speaking as a government employee *in a foreign country* could easily be interpreted as speaking *for* the government. Just don't go there.

"What are you Americans thinking, electing that man!?" she exclaimed.

The table was silent for a moment. About half of the group was American — all government employees.

"You should not have elected him!" she further pressed.

*Some* kind of response was called for and I stepped up to the plate.

"About half the voters would agree with you," I said, which didn't commit us to a political persuasion and didn't reveal our opinions.

She, grunted, left, and we continued our dinner.

## Strong Leaders

I had many casual discussions with my Russian colleagues. I discovered that Russians respect a strong leader. Their history has been rife with them — most notably Joseph Stalin. They would rather have a strong leader doing bad things than a weak leader doing good things — at least it appeared that way. Their respect for strong leaders, however, transcended national boundaries — and gender. Judith DePaul, who is an American woman, was respected by the Russians I knew. So was Madeline Albright, the U.S. Secretary of State at the time, because she had a strong personality. The subsequent rise of Vladimir Putin was not a surprise to me, given the Russian respect for strong leaders.

Part of this is national pride. Although prideful arrogance was not much in evidence in my dealings with Russian colleagues, there was undoubtedly a sense of vulnerability at suddenly being "demoted" from the status of a superpower that the world feared — to a country floundering to figure out how to survive in an unfamiliar world. This is one reason that interest in Western things was so much in evidence. The West was the "winner," so they must have something going for them. "How can we tap into that?" As time went on and the "magic" of Western things did not bring about immediate improvement, disillusion began to occur — and a longing for the "old days" when at least they knew what to expect, however bad. (I see the same dynamic play out in America, where people long for the "good old days" — which upon closer inspection also had a lot of significant problems.)

This created an environment conducive to Vladimir Putin asserting strong leadership. "Make Russia Great Again" was, in essence, his message. This meant riding rough shod over opponents, former Soviet Republics, and even the West in pursuit of that vision. Russians tolerate that because they feel they are on a winning team, even though increasingly it meant returning to the old "familiar" days of state control over freedoms. And the more Putin exerts control, the less possible it is to exert freedoms, especially when part of that control is over the press; he controls the message.

Putin's ascent was after my time in Russia. However, where there are leaders, there are jokes — even in Russia. In 1996, a presidential election was being held, and two of the principal candidates were Boris Yeltsin and Gennedy Zyuganov. Yeltsin, the incumbent president, was running as an independent (but was referred to as being a democrat) and Zyuganov was running as a communist. The joke was: "The democrat is running against the communist, only Yeltsin is not the democrat and Zyuganov is not the communist."

## Russian Time

Russians moved at a different pace than what we were used to. The pace directly correlated to how much attention you paid to what they were doing. If you weren't on site and reminding them of what your priorities were, they would assume their own — and not tell you that they were waiting for your input. Many on the American team thought that by creating a document and getting the Russians to agree to it, that was what would happen. Not necessarily. The Russians themselves told me that when they worked with Germans, the Germans sent a team to be on site and that was an indication that it was important to them, so the Russians paid attention to their requirements. The American team wasn't there, so it must not be important. As I represented the American team, it was important that I be there as much as possible. However, there was a problem. Whenever I was there it was an "event." It could detract from them actually doing work while they dealt with me being there. So I had to balance the two things. I settled on a routine of being on site about two weeks out of every two months — so I was in Russia about 25% of the time between 1995 and 1999. It was enough time to goose along the priorities with enough time away to allow the work to progress.

One of the Boeing engineers, Dr. Robert Rackl, was an Austrian-born engineer who lived in Washington State. Robert worked with Dr. Steve Rizzi on the cabin-noise experiment. On one of his visits he laid out to me his plans for the next two weeks. He had it all mapped out and proudly proclaimed that the Russians had agreed to it, so it was going to happen. I just shook my head and said, "Good luck."

He was incensed. "But they agreed to it. It will happen." He didn't understand my concern. By the end of the two weeks he was very frustrated, because things had not progressed according the "agreement."

There were a lot of reasons for this. For one thing, the Russian team was not getting paid. They also had resource problems. Basic materials required to do the job were not always readily available. There were also just plain old human dynamics. If they didn't like you, things were less likely to get done — and the Russians didn't really like Robert. His frustration translated to harsh words and they would get their backs up. Steve, in contrast, working the same experiment, joked with them, engaged them in conversation about various topics (not all work-related), accepted their ribbing, and generally charmed them. They would bend over backward to help him out. You catch more flies with honey . . .

## Swiss

Once when I was flying to Russia, my seatmate was an American who was on his way to Saudi Arabia. He was a business negotiator who was hired by the Swiss to deal with the Saudis in their place. The cultural gap between the two countries was just too great. The Saudis were all about relaxing, getting to know you on a personal level, developing trust, and taking the time to know who they were dealing with. The Swiss, by contrast, were all business: Get in. Deal. Get out. It was oil and water. The Swiss were like horses chafing at the bit to get it done while the Saudis were still feeling them out. It would actually take longer because the Saudis would not move forward until they got a feel for who they were dealing with. So the Swiss hired a surrogate to do their negotiations for them.

## GPS Trouble

One day I was sitting in my hotel room reading the *Moscow Times* — an English language Moscow newspaper. Buried in it was an article about a Qualcomm engineer who was arrested for taking GPS measurements outside of a former secret Soviet military base. The blood drained from my face. I had been doing exactly the same thing — only *on* a former Soviet military base. One of our experiments required us to know the exact altitude the Tu-144 was above a runway on landing — to measure ground effect (the extra cushion of lift that an airplane experiences when floating just above the ground). The Russian radar altimeter was not working so I had installed a GPS unit on the plane and another on the ground. This combination allowed us to correct errors that we would have were we using one unit by itself.

Every day I was driven into the base — with me holding a portable GPS unit in my hand. I'd wave at the guard and we would drive through.

This, by the way, was another peculiarity. When we entered the base, the Russians in the van would get out, go inside and sign in, and exit inside the fence. I, as an American, would stay in the van, drive through the gate and wait for the Russians to get back in the van. I was never tagged, searched, or otherwise treated as a potential threat.

So when I read the news about the arrest, I was very concerned. I appeared to have done everything the Qualcomm engineer had done — only worse.

Officially, he was arrested for using a GPS unit that had no import license. There was no such thing. The Russians, who were busy starting to reassert control after the Soviet breakup, were writing new directives and rules — some of them retroactive. The Qualcomm engineer was eventually released. The brouhaha subsided, and I was never hassled. It did make me realize how vulnerable I was in an environment that I didn't really understand.

## Religion

One weekend during the summer I was in Moscow with the Langley team. We decided to go visit Zagorsk, a famous site that served as the seat of the Russian Orthodox Church for a long time. We piled into the van and rode out. Michael, our interpreter, had arranged for a tour, which was given by a Russian Orthodox nun who spoke very good English.

I had never encountered a Russian Orthodox nun before, but she resembled Roman Catholic nuns I had met. She was short, confident, and in command. At one point, we were standing in the middle of a large sanctuary and she suddenly upbraided us.

"Look at you!" she exclaimed. "You are standing there with your hands in your pockets, showing disrespect."

Seeing blank looks on our faces, she continued, "If you were talking to your boss, would you have your hands in your pockets?"

We looked at each other, shrugged, and nodded. She was shocked.

"I thought Americans had more manners than that!" she said, shaking her head sadly.

Now, I have to say I did not have my hands in my pockets. I somehow instinctively knew that wasn't a good idea, but I didn't overtly recognize that it was out of respect. But what this incident brought home to me is that we all have cultural expectations that are sometimes not met when we meet someone of a different culture. It happens when we least expect it and are sometimes shocked — whereas the other person is befuddled by our shock. It simply doesn't occur to them that what they are doing is unusual — to you. It further reminded me that we are all ambassadors when we travel abroad, whether we like it or not. Our words and actions can drive people's impressions of all Americans. I know that I was the first American that many I worked with in Russia had ever met. We had many conversations where they asked about how things were done in America. How I comported myself was important. I could have a lasting impact on how all Americans are viewed.

Sometimes when wandering around Moscow I would encounter Americans. This started to happen more frequently in the later years of the program. Once, I was with my interpreter Michael when we ended up in a line behind an American family — who were missionaries. I talked with them a while, but Michael was strangely quiet. Once we parted he vented.

"I hate missionaries coming here. We have our own religion — Russian Orthodox!" The Western protestant worldview is different than that of many in the countries they go to. Michael viewed this as a cultural invasion more than a theological one.

It is important to *understand* the culture you are operating in — especially if you are seeking to change it.

# Chapter 16

# Squeezing Data out of the System

### The Two Geniuses

Although I shared no common language with my hosts, I could often communicate with my counterpart via drawings. Two electrical engineers approaching the same problem and a piece of paper revealed that we often worked the same way.

We saw the same solutions. Our minds worked the same way. Electrons are electrons. Professor Poukhov referred to Sasha and me as "his two geniuses." I chose to take that as a compliment.

### Armenian Sensors

I have mentioned that some of the Russian sensors had peculiarities, like ratiometric calibrations, that we were not used to dealing with, at least for a number of decades. The ones that gave me the most trouble were the airdata sensors. Airdata sensors measure the pressure of the atmosphere surrounding the plane (static pressure) and the pressure created by the plane passing through the air (dynamic pressure). The difference between these two pressures yields an indication of the speed that the plane is moving through the air — its indicated airspeed.

The sensor the Russians were using on the Tu-144LL was composed of a coarse and a fine channel. While the coarse channel would continue to increase its count output as the altitude increased, the fine channel output was more like a sawtooth over the same altitude excursion; it increased for a while, then decreased, then increased again, and so on. To properly calibrate the data, I had to dig into the flight data *by hand* and identify exactly where the counting changed direction (the knee points) and apply that segment's calibration. This knee was not always at the same place because the sensor had "hysteresis" — it varied depending on which direction you were approaching the point. Each time you passed through the knee point from the opposite direction, the location of the knee changed slightly. This manual manipulation was a time-consuming process and led to some inevitable discontinuities in the smooth capturing of air data.

When I asked the Russians who made this sensor, they responded, "Armenia." Then they would laugh hysterically. I came to discover that anything made in Armenia was considered by them to be a joke.

I wasn't laughing.

Finally, during the last year of the program I got fed up and designed my own airdata system based on much better sensors that we at Dryden were used to working with. I had to design some electronic interface cards to convert their unique binary serial outputs into a standard ARINC-429 data stream that would interface to the Russian's French data acquisition system. I was able to mount the two assemblies (one static and one dynamic sensor) on small pallets that would "plug and play" on the Russian racks.

They worked beautifully and I never had to do the hand tracking of airdata knee-points ever again.

## Calibration and Data Pipeline

There is an expression that describes a system that is unique, that there is only one of; it is a "one-off." Everything about this program was "one-off." Once we started to roll up our sleeves and dig into the details of how we would collect, calibrate, and transmit flight data, I increasingly realized that every process we had developed at Dryden to collect and process data would not work for this program.

It seemed that every step of the way there was something to prevent me from using the standard Dryden processing systems. There were a number of differences between how the Russians handled their calibrations and how we did. Time code stamping on the data stream also had some peculiarities.

So I had to re-invent the data pipeline. Eventually I got to a point where I bypassed the entire telemetry processing system and created a whole new system that deposited the final result in the Dryden flight data archive. I also figured out how to transmit the raw flight data from my Moscow hotel room directly to my lab at NASA Dryden. That worked until our IT security folks got wind of what I was doing. "You can't do that!" they said. So I had to figure out a different way. "You can't do that either," they said. I always seemed to have to stay one step ahead of them in order to get my job done. I felt like I was being forced to "smuggle" Russian data *into* the U.S.

Due to a number of issues, including a flaky flight recorder, some Russian work on capturing telemetry files on a PC, and a new Internet capability, I eventually started sending flight data back to the States electronically rather than mailing tapes. We still archived the tapes, but the electronic process significantly improved the turn-around time for posting calibrated flight data in the Dryden archive where the U.S. team could access it.

Let me get technical for a bit here to describe the pieces I am about to talk about. Sensor measurements are collected by a data acquisition system that samples each sensor in a regular fashion — creating an output data stream, or telemetry stream, in a format called pulse code modulation (PCM). This telemetry stream is said to be "commutated," or fragmented in a regular, identifiable, pattern. This telemetry stream is either stored on a recorder or transmitted to the ground for display or recording.

In order to make sense out of this recorded data, the telemetry stream must be played through a "de-commutator" which understands the data "map" (which parameters are where relative to the beginning of the data stream, which is defined by finding a specific pattern of *ones* and *zeros* allowing synchronization). Once this is done, the sensor data can be "cracked out" of the data stream. You can then identify the data specific to a given sensor. Once you have this data, you have to apply a calibration equation to it to turn the coded data into commonly understood engineering units — like temperature in degrees Fahrenheit, pressure in pounds per square inch, or altitude in feet.

Calibration tables are created by applying known pressure, temperature, force, or whatever to the sensor and observing its output from the data acquisition system. The output (in PCM "counts") is captured in the table next to its known pressure or other stimulation. This calibration table is input to a numerical program that creates a mathematical equation allowing you to input PCM sensor counts to it and spit out the engineering unit value. This process is known as a "polynomial regression" — creating a mathematical formula from known data.

There were several differences between the way Dryden normally handled calibrations and flight data and the way Tupolev provided them to us, which made them incompatible. The calibration files were in a different format (and units were in Russian); the sensors often used "ratiometric" calibrations that depended on knowledge of the sensor excitation voltage; the recorded PCM telemetry data was in a file format that we did not use; the data acquisition system was a French system that we had no experience with; and the Russian data files were not compatible with the program (called "Draco") that Dryden used to convert the telemetry flight data into the Dryden flight data base archive.

So, as I mentioned earlier, piece by piece I re-invented our entire data pipeline. I wrote programs to convert the calibration data (and translate the Russian units). I wrote the script to plot the calibration data and create the polynomial regression calibration equations. I wrote code to software decommutate the PCM data provided on disk by the Russians. I manually "massaged" the airdata sensor data to account for the uncertain knee-points (hysteresis) where calibration curves changed. I wrote code to "fix" anomalies (like time jumping backward) in time-tagging of data. And I wrote the code to convert the resulting calibrated data to the format required to archive the data at Dryden. The only thing that was in common with standard Dryden process was the capture and processing of GPS data — as we used our own Ashtech Z-12 systems for the Tu-144LL.

I probably should say that my "cowboy" approach to solving the problem of sucking the Russian data into the Dryden archive did not endear me to some folks at Dryden that felt I should have used their skills, but I found it easier and quicker to write the code myself than to try to explain it or write interface documents so that others could understand what needed to be done. This was partly because of the challenges of coordinating things between the Russian and American teams. I was in a position to understand all the pieces and ask about those that were unclear — in real time.

# Chapter 17

# Flights and Pilot Study

## Flights

There were ultimately 27 test flights in the program.[1] Just over half of them were supersonic flights. The rest were aircraft, system, or pilot check flights.

One of the experiments required us to take pressure measurements at several places along the wing chord. As it would be very difficult to put pressure sensors at each location, we used flexible tubing that would connect the open end (measurement point) of the tube with sensors on the other end inside the plane. However, fastening this tubing to a wing in a manner that the attachment didn't disturb the airflow was a challenge — one in which we were not entirely successful. Dryden had developed an adhesive technique for this on our supersonic aircraft and we passed along the technique information to the Russians. They performed their own tests and found our technique wanting, so they modified it to apply the tubing to the Tu-144LL wing.

All seemed to be going well until one flight, when at Mach 2 the tubing peeled right off and wrapped around the pressure rakes (that stick up into the airflow) at the aft end of the wing. While the adhesive worked very well, it had low shear strength — meaning that once one end started to peel back, it would peel the whole length like opening a zipper. The solution was to apply a strap at the forward end to prevent the peeling from

---

[1] See appendix D for a listing of the Tu-144LL flights.

starting. Using just one strap in that location minimized the airflow disturbance aft of it.

## Pilots

Toward the end of the contracted program, we managed to get it extended for another several months. An experiment was added to have two American NASA pilots fly the Tu-144LL and do a qualitative evaluation of its flying qualities.[2] Gordon Fullerton, a former NASA astronaut and current Dryden research pilot; and Rob Rivers, a Langley pilot, both wangled for this experiment. Gordo really worked hard to make it happen. Rob was every bit as keen. In fact, just a month or two before the scheduled flights, Rob broke his leg. It wasn't completely healed by the time of their flights, but he managed to convince flight surgeons on both sides of the Atlantic to let him fly. Gordo wanted to maximize efficiency by staying near Zhukovsky Air Base rather than having to drive out from Moscow each day. I wasn't sanguine about that since I had tried the same thing before and Judith had shot it down. But Gordo was not to be dissuaded, and as a result they arranged to stay in what turned out to be a retirement home for KGB agents. It didn't turn out exactly as Gordo wanted, because the interpreters still had to come from Moscow each day and they had to wait for them to show up; but it did give them all a unique experience. I gather that menu planning was sometimes them flapping their arms to indicate that they wanted chicken.

I did not go on this trip. By this time I knew I needed to stay in the Moscow hotel because I needed the Internet access;

---

[2] *A Qualitative Piloted Evaluation of the Tupolev Tu-144 Supersonic Transport*, by Rivers, Jackson, Fullerton, Cox, and Princen, NASA TM-2000-209850, February 2000

communication with the U.S. was key to what I was doing. I didn't want to split the interpreters or Tupolev's attention. The pilot team was going to require a lot of attention.

Some years later, Gordo was assigned as project pilot for the Stratospheric Observatory for Infrared Astronomy (SOFIA) aircraft, and we had to travel to Waco, Texas for a flight readiness review (FRR) board. I was serving on the FRR board, which was tasked with reviewing project documents, hearing presentations by the project team, and talking to those who were modifying the aircraft for the upcoming experiments. The modification was a large one that involved cutting a huge hole in the side of the Boeing 747SP aircraft and changing the structural configuration to account for it.

One morning, Gordo and I were having breakfast together at the hotel. The TV was on and they were presenting a breaking story about a NASA astronaut who had driven from Texas to Florida to confront — and possibly kill — a rival for her boyfriend's affections. In order to drive straight through, she had allegedly worn a diaper used by astronauts in space. It was a juicy story involving two astronauts, an affair, and a female Air Force captain.

Gordo watched this news story with a jaundiced eye, but said nothing.

Later that morning, Gordo got up to do his presentation to the FRR.

"Good morning," he deadpanned, "My name is Gordon Fullerton and my previous assignment was as an astronaut. I should tell you that I never drove across the country wearing a diaper."

## Neil Armstrong

One day in 2011, as I was distractedly walking out of my office, I nearly ran into someone coming in. I looked up — and there stood Neil Armstrong! He was looking for the Center Director, and my office was in the suite that used to be the Center Director's office when Neil worked there in the early 1960s. Neil was there this day as part of a National Science Foundation commission to evaluate the state of flight research — which was perceived by many to be not supported well in the political environment of the time. Neil shared that view.

Later, the commission was given a tour of Dryden, and I tagged along. One of the stops was the X-48 cockpit used to remotely pilot the flight vehicle. It also functioned as a flight simulator and members of the commission were offered the opportunity to fly a simulated mission. Neil eagerly stepped into the cockpit and quickly adapted to the unfamiliar controls. After he successfully landed the "vehicle," I stepped in and also "flew" it. Taking the controls and, thankfully, successfully landing the simulated vehicle, I thought to myself *I just trained in flying an aircraft with Neil Armstrong!*

Ok, so it's a stretch — but it's as close as I would ever come to it.

## Enterprise/Jetstar

In the late 1970s, the Space Shuttle *Enterprise* was undergoing flight tests at Dryden and there were two flight crews: Fred Haise and Gordon Fullerton together trained as one crew and Dick Truly and Joe Engle trained as the other. Engle also flew the X-15 about ten years before.

At the time, I was flying as instrumentation engineer on research flights of our Jetstar (C-140), which was an executive jet converted for research purposes. For safety reasons, we would suit up in Nomex (flame retardant) flight suits. I would go to the pilots' "ready room" to change out of my street clothes and into my flight suit and boots.

As I was suiting up one day, Joe Engle comes in, sits down on the bench next to me, and suits up for a Space Shuttle training flight.

*Wow!* I thought. *I have made to the big leagues!* I may be the water boy, but it did feel good to be in the company of major leaguers — doing the same mission prep.

The Jetstar was used for several projects, including a laminar flow control experiment. Around 1980, two different aerospace companies — Lockheed and Douglas — built wing gloves with either tiny slots or tiny holes in them. Pressurized systems in the cabin would feed these holes to expel air with the goal of modifying the flow over the wing section. The Holy Grail here was to achieve laminar, or smooth, flow of air over the wings which would reduce drag and thereby improve aircraft performance. I designed the data acquisition system on board that would assist the on-board researchers in controlling the flow as well as collect "snapshots" of the data. The systems were based on LSI-11 computers and used what was then new technology of bubble memories to store the data. I flew on board to activate and babysit the system.

This project spanned the coasts of the country. The NASA Langley Research Center in Virginia also participated, and one memorable time when we had a meeting back there, the crew reconfigured the aircraft to take out the research pressure distribution system (which looked like beer kegs) and put back in the passenger seats. We then used the plane for its original purpose — as an executive jet — to fly back to Virginia. The project participants back there needed to see the aircraft, so using it for travel served two purposes.

The plane was to be flown by our own NASA pilots. I believe Don Mallick was the pilot, but we were short of pilots to fly second seat and they called Bruce Peterson back from vacation to complete the cockpit staffing.

Bruce was famous, both in the flight-testing community and, in a way, in Hollywood. There was a TV show a few years prior called *The Six Million Dollar Man*. The opening sequence of that show showed a NASA lifting body aircraft crash-landing in the desert. The aircraft rolled several time before coming to a rest. It looked bad — real bad — and it was the premise for the TV show's character losing his legs, arm, and an eye and then being rebuilt into a cyborg that cost six million dollars.

Bruce was the pilot of that actual crash. It didn't kill him or cause limb amputations, but he did lose an eye subsequently due to an infection. He eventually took on the job of Center Safety Officer, but still flew on occasion.

We called him our "six dollar man."

So we are standing by the aircraft, all ready to fly to Virginia — and waiting for Bruce. Soon we spied a slight figure stomping toward the aircraft. The black eye patch identified him as being Bruce. The stubbly growth of beard gave evidence to his having been on vacation. The surly look told us that he wasn't happy about being called back.

As he stomped up to the Jetstar, he glared at it and said, "Two wings, engines, landing gear. OK, checklist complete. Let's go."

With that he mounted the stairs and disappeared into the cabin. We grinned at the absurdly short preflight inspection and climbed aboard.

We ended our meetings in Virginia at 4:30 p.m. a few days later and re-boarded the aircraft to fly back to California. We had to alter course to avoid a pretty solid thunderstorm front that was in our way. Even with that, and winds that are generally against you flying west, we managed to arrive back at Edwards Air Force Base in California before the sun went down that day.

As we approached the landing strip, I realized that Bruce was flying the plane. A thought suddenly occurred to me.

*The plane I am on is being landed by a one-eyed pilot!*

And the other eye was not bionic.

## Celebrities

March and April of 1981 was a memorable period for me. Shortly after a project that I worked on in support of the landing phase of the Space Shuttle (more on that later), I went on a scheduled month-long vacation to the South Pacific. A pass that I bought for Continental Airlines allowed me to fly almost anywhere in that area and I mapped out a route that included Hawaii, Fiji, Australia, New Zealand, Tonga, and Samoa.

I was traveling alone, and met a lot of Australians in Fiji — it being to them as the Caribbean is to many Americans. Since I was a SCUBA diver, I arranged to join a day trip out to one of the small islands, diving on the way. They took us to a small, native village where we sat on the ground and ate with the villagers — thoroughly enjoying ourselves. I got my first taste of Kava, a sort of nerve-numbing drink made from a plant found there.

A few weeks later, I was in American Samoa and I ran into a school teacher who told me that her apartment building, which housed teachers and doctors, had problems with their phone system their landlords wouldn't fix. I decided to take a look. Whereas I did not have my tools of the trade with me (principally a voltmeter), I cobbled together a crude continuity tester by hacking into my flashlight and attaching to it some clip leads that I had. Using this setup I was able to identify several bad connections and fixed them with my knife's blade and screwdriver. Presto, some of the doctors could now receive calls requesting medical attention.

Later, looking out the window of my hotel room, I saw a man who looked familiar, sitting by the pool. *That looks like Buzz Aldrin*, I said to myself.

Then I looked again. *That IS Buzz Aldrin!*

Having been glued to the TV in 1969 like half the planet, I had watched Buzz and Neil Armstrong walk on the moon — and here he was, at *my* hotel in Samoa, of all places.

I couldn't resist. I put on my NASA hat and went down to the pool.

"Colonel Aldrin?" I asked him.

"Yes."

"My name is Glenn Bever and I am very glad to meet you," I said, stretching out my hand.

He took it, and we had a pleasant conversation for ten minutes or so. He asked about my binoculars, which were small but powerful — and borrowed them to look through. (I still have them.) It turned out that he was there with his son — and had just come from Fiji, where he had also been SCUBA diving. We were both in Samoa looking for dive spots. There weren't any.

We parted company, and I thought I would probably never see him again.

The next month, I was back at Dryden, helping with Space Shuttle landing activities. This, the first Shuttle landing from space was a real media event. This would be the first American space mission in six years — and the first to return to a landing strip instead of splashing down in the ocean.

Dryden is a pretty small center, having fewer than 500 employees at the time. So many news media wanted to be there that we had a whole building constructed to house them. (When they left, it became our auditorium and cafeteria.)

When the day of the landing rolled around, there were more media people there than worked at the Center! Many of them were prowling around, looking for someone to interview. Even I got snagged.

However, my job that day was to tell celebrities where to go.

There were more VIPs invited than we had facilities to deal with, so they erected a large, circus-style tent to keep them out of the sun — and serve them food.

Getting on the Air Force base was not trivial, though. So we arranged to have VIPs go to the "old Sears parking lot" in Lancaster, get on chartered buses (there were 40 of them), be driven to the Antelope Valley Inn, get badged, get back on their bus, and be driven out to the base.

This worked pretty well. As I say, my job was to meet the buses arriving at the AV Inn, get on the bus, and tell the VIPs where to go get their badges — and in general what the drill was.

One of the buses arrived, and Buzz Aldrin got off. As I had just talked to him a few weeks previously, I felt comfortable in re-introducing myself. He was talking with two other men, but his eyes lit up and he enthusiastically shook my hand. He remembered me.

"Hey, guys, this is the guy I met in Samoa last month. He's a diver."

He had just introduced me to General William Anders, who was the command module pilot on Apollo 8 — the first manned mission around the moon — and the astronaut who took the iconic photo of the earthrise from lunar orbit; and *Scott Carpenter*, the second American to orbit the Earth in *Aurora 7* — right after John Glenn's flight.

It turns out all three (plus me) were SCUBA divers and we chatted about diving and motion sickness. Scott had participated in several Navy long-term diving studies after he left the astronaut corps and was up on the latest research.

*What's wrong with this picture?* I thought to myself. *One of these men is not like the others.* I was in rarified company indeed.

As one of the last buses arrived at the Inn, I approached the bus to do my spiel — again. But to my surprise and astonishment, a lithe figure jumped off the bus and strode happily over to me, stuck out his hand and said in a very recognizable voice:

"Hi, Glenn. I'm John Denver!"

He was.

What I was trying to figure out in my stupor was *how did he know my name*? The answer was quickly apparent to me; I was wearing my NASA flight jacket, which had my name on the front.

I recovered and started to go into my spiel when he waved a hand and said, "Oh, I have people for that," and proceeded to chat with me for some time about the weather, the landing, and other light subjects.

But he was pleasant, personable, and was perfectly happy chatting with me. He was an aviation and space enthusiast — and I had seen him before, both in concert and in the back of a post-flight debrief for a Space Shuttle Approach and Landing test a few years before. This was the first time I had talked to him, though.

The landing time was approaching, however, so when the time came for his bus to leave, I boarded so that I could get out to the landing site myself. As I sat down, I noticed a man sitting in front of me, wearing a stocking cap. I looked more closely; it was Leonard Nimoy! In front of him was John Denver, his brother, and John's wife Annie (of "Annie's Song").

The ride out to the base took about 45 minutes, and the VIPs gathered in a big tent area — which was out on the lakebed. I was free at that point to wander around the Center and watch the landing from places I knew to be good viewing points.

After the landing I went to the VIP area and saw many other well-known people — including Roy Rogers, a cowboy actor/singer iconic to my generation who was there in full Western regalia, fringes and all.

On another occasion, Jacques Yves-Cousteau was visiting the Center. Cousteau was famous for inventing the SCUBA tanks and regulators that most divers used and also for the adventures in his research ship RV *Calypso*. Everyone in my generation had heard of him and watched his occasional programs on TV. John Denver had even written a song about *Calypso*. When I learned to SCUBA dive — and particularly when I was on college trips diving in the Bahamas on the RV *Dragonlady* — I would imagine myself being part of Cousteau's crew on the *Calypso*.

Cousteau was at Dryden to watch one of the lifting body flights, the X-24B, piloted by John Manke. As was customary, many of us would go to the roof of the building to watch flights. On this day I found myself standing right next to Cousteau and experiencing the flight vicariously right along with him. When he was told of the X-24B's landing speed, he was amazed and repeated in his signature thick French accent: "Two hundred miles per hour?"

After the X-24B landed, Cousteau was driven out to the lakebed to see the craft and meet the pilot as he got out of the cockpit. When Manke climbed out, he was wearing swim fins! Cousteau doubled over in laughter. When the ground crew climbed up to assist Manke after landing, they had handed him the fins and helped him change his footwear, secreting his flight boots away — setting the stage for the incongruous sight of a pilot in the desert deplaning wearing swim fins.

## Jerry Ross

Nearly half of the Space Shuttle landings were at Edwards. They continued to attract a lot of attention and we had a steady stream of VIPs on site at Dryden for many landings. As a result, they still needed Dryden employees to help with escort duty, and I did a lot of it.

As time went on, the special guests were usually just the families of the astronauts in the Shuttle — and their friends. I would remain with them throughout much of the day and answer questions, point out things of interest, escort them to viewing areas, and just generally hang out with them.

This was fun duty. I got to meet many excited family members and often find out many lesser-known facts about the astronauts from a perspective only a family member can give. However, it also added to my personal sense of tragedy when the *Challenger* exploded on launch because I had met Judith Resnik's parents and sister and also talked with Ellison Onizuka; Resnik and Onizuka were two of the astronauts who died in *Challenger*. At the time, Ellison complained to me that there was "a long line in Houston" to get on a Shuttle flight manifest. Tragically, he got his chance.

During one landing activity, I was sitting in the conference room chatting with one of the astronaut families. We were discussing the re-entry process when the man sitting in front of us turned around and started telling us how he handled reentry.

He was Jerry Ross — a Shuttle mission specialist who had been on several missions and ultimately tied the record for most space missions by an astronaut — seven!

Jerry was very personable and unassuming, but we were fascinated by his account of *standing up* during most of the re-entry. He would stand and peer out the window through the upper reentry — when the Shuttle was decelerating from Mach 25 down to subsonic, only strapping into his seat for landing. He claimed this helped him re-acclimate to a 1 g environment more quickly than remaining in his seat the whole time. Re-acclimation is one of the problems that astronauts must deal with after being in space for any length of time.

For long-term space studies, they would take astronauts off the Shuttle in stretchers (hidden inside of people-movers because it looked bad hauling them off that way) and wheel them to the dispensary for study before they stood up. I got to observe this part of the operation close up sometimes when I would take a family member out to greet them before they were trucked into the dispensary. The astronaut usually looked tired but excited to see their loved ones after such a thrilling space journey.

During this whole period of early Space Shuttle landings, you never knew who was going to show up at Dryden. You would hear pages for celebrities, many of which were probably hoaxes, in which some wit had called the paging number and requested a page. So when you heard "Will Farrah Fawcett Majors please call extension 3747," you were never really sure if it was a joke or if the famous actress were actually on site.

# Chapter 18

# Travel and Free Time

## Metro

What do you do for fun on a weekend in Moscow? Well, for me it was often walking around town watching people and seeing sights. I would often encounter classical string quartets playing in the subterranean walkways heading into the local subway system — or Metro. These world-class musicians were either out of work or taking advantage of a "business" opportunity (playing for money on the street). The environment couldn't have been good for the sensitive string instruments, however, so I doubt they did it on a lark.

I gained quite a bit of proficiency in using the Metro. It was extensive, but poorly marked. While they had Red Lines, Blue Lines, etc. all nicely marked on Metro schematics, the subways themselves did not use color *anywhere*. The Metro directions were marked only with lists of stop names — in Cyrillic — and the names were long. Being able to read Cyrillic Russian when I traveled the Metro was really helpful.

The escalators in the Metro station traveled at warp speed. Ok, not *that* fast but probably two or three times the escalator speeds that I had experienced elsewhere. So as you're whizzing down the escalator trying to read the long Cyrillic names to see what platform to go to; clearing your ears, which are popping from the altitude change; and trying to keep from tripping at the bottom — you are busy. I often fantasized about taking cans of colored paint into the Metro stations to paint lines on the wall or floor — or even the Metro signs — so that the uninitiated could more reasonably navigate. However, this was probably the point; the Russians in Soviet times had no desire for the uninitiated to be able to navigate around Moscow via Metro. It's a security issue.

Entering the Metro station, you would go through gates that were controlled by dropping *jeton*s (tokens) into the slot. These were round plastic "coins" that you bought. *Jeton*s were reusable. However, Russians discovered that they could shave a piece of ice and drop it into the slot — achieving entry — and so the gates were redesigned to accept paper tickets instead. Not as romantic.

The Metro stations themselves are rather opulent. Marble floors, large statues, and even chandeliers are evident. These were the pride of Soviet public works. The subway cars themselves were boxy, no-frills, and functional — like most Russian technology. They got you there.

## Ishmylova

So . . . weekends. What did I do besides wander around town and catch up on sleep? I went to the Ishmylova flea market.

This involved a Metro ride to nearly the last stop on the line, but I enjoyed wandering around looking at the wares people would bring. The booths were filled with arts, crafts, military hardware, and trinkets. My favorites were Russian матрёшка (matryoshka) stacking dolls and hand-made передники (peredniki), or aprons. I got really good at spotting good quality work for low prices. They were small and easy to carry in my already overloaded luggage. They made good gifts, too. I bought from the artists who made them. Most of these people had other jobs, but this was a way to make money — hard currency — on the weekends. It was a new experience for Russians, and they took to it.

## Shorts

When the Langley cabin noise experiment team first came to Moscow, I gave them detailed information about what to expect from the time their flight arrived at Sheremetyevo to getting to the hotel. I also gave them instructions about what to wear to blend in when touring Moscow the first weekend they were there.

I suggested that they wear plain shirts, dark pants, and dark, non-athletic shoes. When I met them in the lobby, I saw that they had followed my instructions to the T. They were wearing plain shirts, dark shoes . . . and shorts! OK, the shorts were dark, but *shorts*! They weren't going to blend. Nobody in Moscow wore shorts. It never occurred to me to specify *long* pants.

## Bolshoi

On one of my flights out of Moscow I saw something that caught my attention. There was an unusually large group of attractive, lithe, young women who seemed to group around an older, distinguished looking, white-haired man. They congregated in the lounge at the airport and then in the aircraft's galley area during the flight. Later I learned that it was the Bolshoi Ballet Company, including the director (the white-haired man). They were going on tour in the United States. I had probably seen many of these dancers performing when I had gone to a performance in the Bolshoi Theater previously. By the way, there is also a Маленький (Malenki) Theater next to the Bolshoi. Вольшой (Bolshoi*)* means "big" in Russian. *Malenki* means "little."

## Baby Flight

In the late 1990s, Moscow was a popular destination for couples wanting to adopt children. Russia had a lot of orphans and Russian authorities were (usually) OK with Americans adopting. I personally know two couples that did so. It was not uncommon to find myself on a "baby flight." These were flights out of Moscow that had a number of new parents bringing their adopted infants home to the U.S. On one memorable flight I was completely surrounded by babies. I had one on each side, one in the row in front of me, and one behind — not to mention the 20 or so other babies on the plane. So picture this: a plane full of brand new, inexperienced parents holding babies who until a few days before were strangers. The plane is undergoing normal pressure changes. The babies are fussing and crying — a lot — and the parents have no idea how to interpret or deal with their displeasure. They can't move around, and they can't quiet the babies. Wide-eyed and frantic, they are embarrassed by their lack of expertise and apologetic regarding the comfort of their fellow passengers — such as me. The new mother next to me kept apologizing. I just philosophically shrugged my shoulders and relaxed — soaking in the chorus and feeling sorry for the parents.

## Turkish Delight

I often had meetings in Europe for another activity I was working on at the same time I was working on the Tu-144LL project. One of these meetings took me to Turkey. For efficiency, I was going to fly on to Moscow after the meetings there were done.

But I had a complication. Entry into Russia required a visa which had to be applied for in advance. There was a delay in processing mine and I would not receive it until I was already in Turkey. So we arranged for the visa to be sent to my Turkish hotel. While staying in the hotel in Ankara, Turkey, we had a bomb scare. It turns out that there was a Bosnian convention being held in the same hotel, and they were the target. This was during the Bosnian war in the 1990s.

There turned out to be nothing to it, however, but it kept me distracted from my other worry. My visa had not arrived and I was running out of time. Each day I would check at the desk. No visa. Finally it was time to check out. Still no visa. I asked if it could have been delivered someplace else. They went to a back storage room and, voila! My visa came back in his hand.

Just in the nick of time! I left for the airport in a taxi, which cost over one million Turkish lire. (There were a lot of zeros on that banknote.) After boarding my plane, I settled in with a sigh of relief. My relief was short-lived because I looked down at the tarmac and saw my luggage sitting there in a pile with others. I saw no indication that it was going to be put on the plane. I got increasingly antsy and finally asked a flight attendant about it.

"You need to put your luggage in the luggage compartment, sir." So I dashed off the airplane and did that.

OK, *now* I can relax — although my seatmate was a very wide Russian. I looked around the airplane and noticed that most of the passengers were Japanese. Small Japanese. So I am sitting there leaning to the side to make room for the girth of my seatmate — but I am on the plane. I have my visa. My luggage is with me. OK.

The plane took off. It was a Tupolev passenger airliner. The "no smoking" sign turned off and immediately the entire Japanese contingent lit up cigarettes and the cabin filled with smoke. I don't do well with smoke under normal circumstances, but a plane full of smoke is torture. Then the smoke detectors went off and they illuminated the no smoking sign again. Out went the cigarettes and after a while the air cleared somewhat. Off went the no smoking sign. Again everyone lit up. Smoke detector — and the cycle repeated.

Fortunately, the flight from Ankara to Moscow was a relatively short one. We landed in weather that was a cold drizzle. By the time I deplaned and got to my hotel I was coming down with a cold. Sigh.

This was one of my less pleasant trips.

# Chapter 19

# Other Russians

Sometimes I would come face to face with relics of the Cold War. Strolling down the hall on Zhukovsky air base I spied a bulletin board with a cartoon sketch that was some kind of notice. Drawn to it I discovered what it was. It told people what to do in case of a nuclear attack — from the United States! It was a stark reminder of our spotty history with each other. I remembered similar posters when I was a boy in the United States. The message was the same, but the enemy was reversed.

## Sperny

Across the hall from that bulletin board was Mr. Sperny's office. As head of the calibration lab, his office was near to the lab space that we frequently used. We often ate lunch there, whether or not Mr. Sperny was in. One day we were having lunch there and chatting when I mentioned that Mr. Sperny reminded me of a guy back at Dryden named Bill, "only Mr. Sperny is a communist and Bill is a redneck," I said.

The Russians' eyes got big and they asked me apprehensively, "How did you know that Sperny is a communist?"

I jerked my thumb to the wall and said, "He has a picture of Lenin hanging in his office."

We never ate in Sperny's office again.

## Bad Manners

One day, Wilson Vandiver and I were at the Tupolev Business Center, which was a very nice addition built onto the Tupolev main building in Moscow. After the experiences with the decayed infrastructure, this new wing is where they brought all foreign visitors. Nice conference rooms; a little kitchenette where the "protocol girls" made tea and served biscuits; nice, functioning, and clean restrooms. On this day, I stayed late and Wilson returned to the hotel by Metro with our interpreter. Wilson was chatting away — in English — and an older Russian lady on the Metro accosted him. She started scolding him, although Wilson didn't know that. He just smiled at her, confused. *Maybe she doesn't like my tie*, he thought. The car arrived at the next stop and she got off. Then a young Russian man came up and repeated the performance. Wilson was thoroughly confused by now and asked the interpreter what the problem was. He was reluctant to tell him, but finally relented. It seems that they were objecting to his body posture.

"You should be ashamed of yourself, crossing your legs on the subway. You are an intellectual. You should know better!" she had said. The young man had said much the same thing. All right, I suppose she thought that Wilson was an intellectual because he was speaking English and dressed nicely. It probably never occurred to her that he was foreign. At that time foreigners riding the Metro was uncommon.

So what was the problem with crossing legs on the subway? The interpreter never would tell Wilson. We talked about it later, and I'm still guessing — but it probably has to do with showing the sole of his foot (his foot was perched horizontally over his knee), which I know in Arab cultures is regarded as an insult. Perhaps it had to do with taking up too much space on the seat.

Maybe it was just considered plain bad manners for obscure reasons.

## Superstitions

Once, our interpreter Michael invited a small group of Americans, including me, to his apartment for dinner. This was a special treat. We had never before been invited into a Russian's home — nor were we ever invited to one after that, for that matter. We were able to meet Michael's wife and son for the first time. Our education on Russian superstitions began before we ever set foot in his apartment, however. One of us thought to buy Michael's wife a dozen roses.

When the door opened, we extended our hands and Michael told us, "It is considered bad luck to shake hands across the threshold. You must come in first."

Then we handed them the roses. Michael observed "Never give a Russian an even number of roses. It is bad luck."

Other superstitions had more serious implications. Donna Gallaher, a technician from NASA Langley, was often in Russia to help install and check out the cabin noise experiment. It was critical that she be onboard the aircraft before the flight to make sure the system was working and deal with any last minute issues. Tupolev did not want her onboard then. It turns out that it is "bad luck" for a woman to be onboard an aircraft before a flight. I had to do a lot of talking at a preflight meeting to get them to relent and let her do her job.

When the American pilots came out to fly the Tu-144LL, we sent a Dryden photographer, Jim Ross, and a Dryden videographer, Lori Losey, out to Russia to film the flights. I had given them detailed instructions regarding how to enter the country, what to do, in general what to expect. While this was very useful to them, I forgot to mention one thing; Lori needed to go onboard the aircraft to film flight preparation activities, and the Russians balked at letting her on board.

## Harassment

Once I found myself in an uncomfortable conversation with a group of Russian women at lunch. Somehow the subject of sexual harassment came up and they were asking me what that was all about.

"Er, well, ahem," I stammered, "It is when someone — usually a man — takes advantage of a position of power to make suggestive remarks or take sexual liberties with someone — usually a woman."

They laughed and shrugged. It was sort of a "So what? What can you do?" kind of laugh. Soviet Russians made great show of equality — the first woman in space, for example. But when you scratch the surface of Russian culture, you find a deeply ingrained view of a woman's place — and it is not equal. I worked with a number of women — technicians, managers, engineers — and it was invariably a good working relationship, but Russian sensitivity to women's rights was closer to the U.S. in the 1960s than it was to modern day America.

Although actions that came to light a few decades later in the U.S. entertainment industry and political arena would indicate that we have not made as much progress as I had thought —nevertheless the *expectation* for many years in the U.S. has been that harassment of women is poor behavior at best. The cultural environment in Russia had not reached even that expectation yet.

# Chapter 20

# Different Encounters

## Customs

You had to be careful going through customs on the way out of Moscow. You know the standard question, "Have you packed your own luggage and has it ever been out of your sight since?" On one occasion, one of my traveling companions answered "no" to the second question and we found ourselves having to open a wooden crate using a coin as a screwdriver just so the Russian customs agent could see inside.

One time, Wilson Vandiver — my predecessor on the program — and I were leaving Moscow and his bag was scanned. They pulled it aside and started going through it. Wilson was nervous because he had a Russian airdata probe he was taking back to the U.S. and he was sure that was what they found on their scan. He had it legitimately, but one never knew what issues might arise. Out came his flotsam and jetsam. More sweat. Then they reached in and took out the airdata probe — set it aside — and continued to look. They finally found whatever had set them to digging through his luggage in the first place, were satisfied, and put everything back — including the airdata probe. Very relieved, Wilson and I gathered our things and headed out.

## Boomed!

The Tu-144LL had to be re-engined. The original engines were no longer in production, so they made some inlet modifications and installed the Kuznetsov NK-321 engines that were normally used on the Tu-160 "Blackjack" bomber. These changed the flight characteristics — adding some performance. One day the Tu-144LL, in supersonic flight, "boomed" the factory in which these engines were manufactured and blew out a number of windows.

That's poetic justice.

## Gorbachev

On one flight to Moscow, I had managed to upgrade to first class using frequent flyer miles. NASA was sensitive of upgrades and it was only recently that the rules changed enough so that I could do that on occasion. It was particularly nice on the very long eight- to nine-hour flights overseas. I am not a short man and not having my knees jammed into the seat in front of me or wrestling for the armrest with my neighbor is a real treat. I arrive in better condition.

On this flight I was dozing a bit when my seatmate leaned over and asked me an odd question: "What is Mikhail Gorbachev's middle name?" I shrugged and went back to dozing.

Later I opened my eyes and ... Mikhail Gorbachev was staring at me! "I must be dreaming," I thought. I closed my eyes and reopened them. He was still there, wine stain birthmark and all. Gorbachev was sitting in the seat right in front of me with his wife, Risa. Later, when we landed and got up to leave, I tried taking a picture unobtrusively, but since I didn't use a flash, all I got was a silhouette. I followed them off the airplane and wasn't paying close attention to where I was going. I was in "follow the guy in front" mode. This was nearly disastrous because they took a left turn into a private area where I would not have been welcomed.

## Medal

During one of my latter trips, Professor Poukhov presented me with a medal "For Excellence in the Field of Aviation Technology." It was a Tupolev medal and he told me it previously had only been awarded to one other foreigner — the head of North Korea! That put me in, well, strange company. What was also amusing to me was this was the first medal I was awarded — by anybody. Subsequently I received three medals from NASA, but this Russian medal was my first.

My interpreter suggested that I not display it on my person. (Russians are fond of doing that — even on civilian clothing.) He didn't tell me why, but I suspect it was because the Russians I worked with might be jealous. This medal was apparently highly regarded and they may have felt that I did not earn it — causing potential drama.

# Chapter 21

# Germans

## German TV

On one of my trips I was joined by a German film crew. They wanted to film a show for The Learning Channel (TLC) about the Tu-144LL program. They wanted to focus on me, since I was the American on site. Nadja Franz was my interviewer and she started with a sit-down interview at the Tupolev Business Center.

The first question she asked was: "So tell me, as an aerospace expert, are you afraid to fly?"

I chuckled and said, "No. The hard part is getting *to* the airport. Once I get on the plane I can relax."

I guess that was a kind of ice-breaker. I relaxed into the interview, which covered things I was comfortable talking about.

They then spent the next three days following me around, filming my interactions with the Russians and the aircraft, and even filmed me wandering around Red Square. There we were confronted by some Russian guards who informed us that to film in Red Square required a permit — and payment. So we moved just off the square — where they were able to get classic Red Square buildings in the background without actually being in Red Square.

With the process of largely filming me just doing my job, it was a sort of reality show before there were such things. The footage went in the can and that's the last I heard about it for a while. The producer later contacted me and told me that the deal with TLC had fallen through. So I figured the program was dead.

Sometime later I was at a meeting with a German colleague and he handed me a videotape. It was a recording of the show, which had aired in Germany. His daughter happened to be recording it and recognized my name, so she saved it for me. The show, of course, was narrated in German, and in PAL format — a European video format which doesn't play on consumer video cassette players typically found in the States. I got it converted to the more common NTSC format by our NASA video group so that I could watch it. I didn't understand German, but my wife did, and she was able to tell me the gist of what they were saying.

A few years after the Tu-144LL program ended, I was visiting an old friend in Germany — my oldest friend; Gary Sowders and I grew up together near St. Louis, Missouri. He was now living in Germany with his German wife and their two young children. I had brought with me a copy of the German TV program (*Konkordski*) that featured me working on the Tu-144LL. As German speakers I thought they might appreciate it. I popped in the tape.

Their son Brian, who was about six or seven years old then, suddenly realized that the guy on the TV he was watching — was *me*. He whipped his head between me on the TV and me on the couch. Then he hopped off his chair and came over to plop himself next to me on the couch, grinning at me.

Brian wanted to go see what he called "your airplane." I then learned that recently a Tu-144 had been installed in the local airplane museum in Sinsheim — which was nearly visible from their house. Brian apparently thought I had designed the plane. (I hated to disabuse him of the notion.) So we went down to the museum and saw it. You could even go inside of it, and for the first time I took video of the inside of a Tu-144. Not "mine," but a similar model.

# Chapter 22

# Who is this Guy?

### Growing Up

My mother has said: "If you had known as a child that you would be going to work for NASA, you could not have waited to grow up." I think she was right.

I was born in 1953, the second of three children born to Robert and Emily Bever. Our birth spacing was all two years apart, with my brother, Joe, being two years older than me and my sister, Theresa, being two years younger. We grew up in Berkeley, Missouri — a suburb of St. Louis in North St. Louis County.

McDonnell Douglas, a large aerospace corporation, had its headquarters in Berkeley, and the St. Louis airport was adjacent to both McDonnell and Berkeley. I grew up seeing and hearing all kinds of aircraft fly overhead. My high school was on the approach path to the airport. Many were the times when a teacher had to pause, wait for the noisy airplane to pass overhead, and then continue a lecture.

Living only a mile from the McDonnell Douglas plant, I got tours there. I saw the production lines of F-4s and F-15s, saw the maiden transatlantic flight of the DC-10, watched the first American space station — Skylab — being constructed in the clean room, and sat in the cockpit of a Gemini space capsule.

In Berkeley, I could go to the store — and elementary school — without crossing a street. The city attorney lived next door. The school board president (and city's first police chief) lived next door to him. His brother lived across the street. It felt like a safe community and I thrived there.

My junior high was across the street from my elementary school, and my high school was a few blocks farther down the street. It was a residential neighborhood and our block was our playground.

None of these schools exist anymore — victims of changing demographics that were exacerbated by the encroachment of both the St. Louis airport and a new freeway. My entire neighborhood is gone. No houses remain — all bought under eminent domain and torn down to build a new freeway. My old front yard is now an onramp to that freeway.

I went to church in Ferguson, which was the city right next door. I often rode my bike the 2 ½ miles to church from my house in Berkeley.

Ferguson at the time was a largely white, fairly affluent community. Berkeley, on the other hand was about 10% black — which was reflected in the racial makeup of my high school. Sandwiched between the two cities was Kinloch, which was a 100% black community and very poor. The way school systems were funded at the time was by the community tax base. Berkeley had a low tax rate because McDonnell Aircraft Corporation was largely located there. Kinloch had a high tax rate because there was no industry there that could subsidize the public services — like schools. This led to a large inequity in school quality and is one of the reasons the Kinloch population had an interest in moving out. As the surrounding communities began to absorb a wider racial mixture, the institutions that served them — such as the police force — often did not keep up with the change. This, I believe, is one of the factors that led to the tragedy that made Ferguson, Missouri a nation-wide household name many years after I left the area.

Our family took annual camping vacations, and we traveled all over the Midwest — with a few trips to the East Coast and the far West. I got very good at packing — and was in charge of loading the simple, utility-free Nimrod tent-trailer that we eventually got after being flooded out of our tent one very rainy night in Kentucky.

We spent many happy hours camping alongside the Current River — a spring-fed river in Southern Missouri that eventually became part of the National Scenic Riverways system. There I learned how to expertly handle an open canoe — and play out scenes from *Tom Sawyer* on a river much smaller than the Mississippi.

My most memorable first achievement was attaining the rank of Eagle Scout. In Boy Scouts, this is the highest rank; and I made it when I was thirteen and a half years old, which was the youngest age possible then. My older brother, Joe, had earned his Eagle the previous year, and my scouting family was proud of both of us. The skills I learned in planning, organizing, and executing activities as well as the exposure I got to different endeavors would set the stage for my life accomplishments. The last merit badge I earned for my Eagle rank was the electricity merit badge.

**Ham Radio**

My interest in electronics started when I was 12 or 13. My brother had received an Edmundson Scientific electronic projects kit, but wasn't really interested in it. So I appropriated it and started putting together all the kits in the manual. The culmination was an 80-meter regenerative receiver. It used three tubes and allowed me to receive some amateur AM radio stations. There weren't many AM ham stations left at that time (1968) — most having converted to single side band (SSB), which was a more efficient but less stable modulation method. But I was able to hear enough stations to whet my appetite.

About the same time that my interest in electronics was growing, I was required to write a term paper in school on some career I might pursue. I mentally flipped a coin between chemical engineering and electrical engineering — and EE won; so I researched that career.

From that moment on I never wanted to be anything else.

I bought an R55A Knight Kit short-wave receiver and assembled it, then spent many hours tuning around and listening to radio stations. It covered frequencies from AM broadcast up through high frequency (HF) ham — with a lot of short-wave radio broadcast stations in between. This was kind of like "surfing" the web in the days before the Internet. I would stumble upon stations from all over the world — including amateur radio stations.

I was hooked. I started keeping a log of stations listened to, bought a Morse Code practice record, and a practice oscillator kit.

I earned my first amateur radio (ham) license when I was 15 years old. After all the short wave listening I did with my Knight Kit, I had become interested, but I didn't know any hams and had no obvious way of plugging into the hobby. However, upon perusing my log book, I found a small number of local hams I had heard. So I wrote a postcard to one and asked if he would be interested in helping me become a ham radio operator. His name was Ed Lowall — W0NIC (his radio call letters). Ed called me and that began a period of radio mentoring that really got me started. Ed was my father's age and the technical director for KSD TV — the St. Louis NBC television station. I spent most Saturday evenings at his house in Ferguson talking about radio, testing tubes, contacting hams on his Swan 350 transceiver, or rendezvousing with other hams at a Steak 'n Shake for a cheeseburger. Ed proctored my Novice class ham license exam and I became radio ham WN0WFQ. He also encouraged me through subsequent testing for my General class and Advanced class licenses (changing my call letters to WA0WFQ), which I earned over the next year or so. He helped me procure my first transmitter, which was an ancient Johnson Viking II — a "battleship" — or seemed to weigh as much as one. It dated from the early 1950s and had no solid state electronics in it at all. Even the diodes were tubes. It was frequency controlled by a crystal — which limited my transmitting but it did enable me to get on the air — along with the R55A receiver.

As it only handled continuous wave (CW — Morse Code) or AM transmissions on fixed crystal frequencies, I soon upgraded to a Heathkit SB-101 transceiver that would handle multiple frequency bands and the new-fangled single-sideband voice transmission. The SB-101 was a kit that I assembled and soldered. I was too cheap to buy the corresponding power supply, so I designed and built one from old TV parts that I had scrounged from what would be called "e-waste" today. I went around the neighborhood and collected old TVs that had been set out on the curb for disposal and cannibalized their parts.

After obtaining my Novice license, I joined the American Radio Relay League (ARRL) and on the cover of the first ARRL *QST* magazine I received there was a picture of a new type of antenna — a Delta Loop beam. I built that 15-meter wavelength antenna and spent many happy hours "working" stations all over the world using it. My mother would joke that I would come out of the basement and tell her about the weather in Germany but not know what the weather was right outside our house.

As my interest and experience grew, I decided to study for commercial class radio licenses. The summer of my junior year I became unemployed — having dropped my 75-cent per hour job as an egg-man to take a $2.25 per hour job at an A&P Amart grocery store, which then laid me off after only a month or so. This left me with no job and half the summer left. In order to be productive I spent the rest of the summer studying for the Second-Class Commercial Radiotelephone License and subsequently passed the FCC exam. This qualified me — legally anyway — to service commercial two-way radios.

I then went for the First-Class Commercial Radiotelephone license — which would allow me to legally be in charge of operations at a commercial radio or TV broadcast station. (I also earned the ship radar endorsement at the same time.) I had become aware of these licenses from my mentor, Ed, who held a First-Class Commercial license for his position at KSD. While I never actually used these licenses for their intended purposes, they made a wonderful addition to my resume and I think were directly responsible for two jobs I subsequently held.

The following summer — while working a very lucrative, but menial, job as a chemical vat stirrer at Mallinckrodt Chemical Works, where my Father worked as a Chemist — I applied for radio jobs at several local stations. One of them actually called me, thinking to offer me a job as a DJ. He quickly discovered that is not where my talents lay, but did offer me a job of "running radials" for a new antenna system they had installed. This entailed my walking straight lines in several directions around the antenna and taking field strength measurements — through cornfields, peoples' back yards, etc. I accepted; it was about a three-day job. I was working the graveyard shift at the chemical plant that week and after getting off shift I would head straight out across the Mississippi River to take the measurements at the station on the Illinois side. I was partnered with a broadcast journalism college student — who was so enamored with that field that he spent the entire time trying to talk me into going into that business.

## The University of Illinois

I applied for entry into the University of Missouri at Rolla, Purdue University, and the University of Illinois at Urbana/ Champaign — and was accepted at all three. I turned down a full scholarship to Rolla in favor of attending my parents' alma mater — the University of Illinois. (Several of my relatives had attended that school and my mother, Emily Frank Bever, was co-valedictorian there in 1947.)

I started attending classes at the University of Illinois in September, 1971. My major was Electrical Engineering in that highly competitive school, and the next five years were grueling for me. Being a serious student, I applied myself to studies and didn't take much time off for recreation. Even my recreation involved classwork when I trained on Saturdays to be a SCUBA diver.

My time at the University of Illinois (U of I) was pretty intense. This was not a "safety" school. At the time of my entry, it was (and remains) a highly regarded university — and routinely is ranked as one of the top five or six electrical engineering programs in the country. I often think of the U of I as the least known top school. MIT, Caltech, Stanford, and Purdue are among other schools that rank in that strata — and most people have heard of them. U of I faculty have, over the years, been key to several innovations — including ground-breaking research and the invention of sound on film, lasers, superconductivity, and the light-emitting diode (LED). One of the faculty members, who had an office right down the hall from mine, was John Bardeen. He is the only person ever to be awarded two Nobel prizes in physics: one for the invention of the transistor and the other for his work in superconductivity.

So the College of Electrical Engineering attracted a lot of bright students, which made the competition to get in — and survive — more challenging. In a nutshell, I had to work my tail off to keep up. I managed to graduate with a GPA of 3.6/4[1] — only succumbing to one "C" in my career (in probability and statistics my last semester, when I was in the full throes of senioritis), and graduated with high honors. Being an introvert and being really focused on learning my craft, I had little time (or frankly, the inclination) to party. My routine was regular. I always got eight hours of sleep. In bed by 11 p.m. and up by 7 a.m. I knew that my worst enemy to learning would be to fall behind on my sleep.

I ate all my meals each week in the dorm cafeteria except for one on Sunday when the cafeteria was closed. I restricted myself to watching TV only on the weekends (a reward I looked forward to).

Engineering school is a chain of educational events. Each builds on the last. If you don't understand one semester of math you will be hard pressed to understand the next level. So I was rigid and disciplined — fearing that to be otherwise would spell disaster.

I didn't make many friends. Running off to California every other semester didn't help in that regard. (More about this later.) It wasn't until my last two semesters that I really made close friends — many of whom I remain in touch with to this day.

---

[1] University of Illinois actually used a 5-point scale instead of the more common 4-point scale. I converted here to the more commonly used scale.

Shortly after I arrived on campus, I was awarded a "work-study" program job opportunity — whereby I could get a University job with 10% of my wages funded by the university and 90% would come from the federally-funded program. *Cafeteria food services, here I come,* I thought.

However, my radio experience and licenses saved me from that. I was offered a position as a lab technician in the physics department — a job normally reserved for upper classmen. I was to hold this job throughout my entire college career whenever I was on campus — even when my work-study award expired. After my freshman year I moved to a dorm right across the street from the Physics Building in which I worked, making it very convenient.

## Capacity 46

Having learned to SCUBA dive my first semester at the university, I was anxious to try it out in some place more exotic than the indoor pool or the local quarry. I got the chance when I saw that the University of Illinois SCUBA diving club was planning a trip to the Bahamas. Perfect.

One of the SCUBA club members owned an old school bus. He and his wife planned to drive this bus to Florida with all the other people going on the trip as passengers. So during the semester break — which was at the end of January at that time — we all piled in and headed for warmer climes to the south.

The trip was uneventful, for a while, and I reveled in thoughts of the upcoming adventure. I had a direct view of a placard in the front of the bus that declared "Capacity 46" was how many people the bus held, and that became my name for the trip.

Halfway between Nashville and Chattanooga, Tennessee, the bus engine cracked a cylinder head. It was finished, but we were on a deadline to catch a plane out of Miami, Florida to Nassau.

We had to be towed to the nearest town, which was Manchester, Tennessee. The first tow truck broke down before it reached us. The second tow truck had no windows, and it was cold outside. Since there wasn't enough room to carry all of us in the truck anyway, we all scrunched down in the bus so as not to be seen, and the truck towed us that way into town.

What to do now? Some of the passengers bailed. They had been just riding to Florida and were not part of the diving group. I heard later that they had gone back to the freeway and tried to hitch, but were picked up by the Tennessee Bureau of Investigation (TBI) for doing that and were deposited at a bus station.

The rest of us started calling rental-car companies from a pay phone. We gathered around the callers, holding out handfuls of change so that they could keep feeding the phones for the long distance calls to both Nashville and Chattanooga. We finally found a company that had cars to rent — and would rent to us. A complication was that you had to be over 21 to rent, and most of us were undergraduates under that age.

Our designated drivers hitched (TBI notwithstanding) into Chattanooga, rented the cars, and drove them back to pick us up. It took three or four cars to squeeze in all of us and our dive gear. Now we began a "suicide run" to Florida. We had lost a lot of time, so we resolved to drive straight through, swapping out drivers. Of course, there weren't enough drivers over the age of 21 to make that work, so we all took turns behind the wheel anyway. I was 18.

My turn came up crossing central Florida. It was the middle of the night, foggy, and I was extremely tired; I started hallucinating. Overpasses would seemingly jump toward me and then jump back. I never experienced anything like that before or since. Due to the fog, it wouldn't take much to overdrive my headlights, but the time pressure made the prospect of slowing down unattractive.

While I was mulling this over, a car passed me going the speed limit. I made a snap decision and accelerated to follow the car, locking my eyes onto his tail lights — and hoping he knew what he was doing.

We arrived at Miami International Airport a half hour before our plane was scheduled to depart. We made it! We piled gratefully onto the plane and flew to Nassau, where we went through customs. I was the first one in — and the last one out. I was the "lucky one" they chose to do a thorough search of, and they tore down my luggage — going through everything. They got very excited when they came across a vial of white powder in my toilet kit. It was saccharin — an artificial sweetener. I told them what it was, but the agent opened it and put some on his tongue. I bet he experienced the intense aftertaste for the rest of the day. In any case they put my luggage back together and shooed me out.

We went straight to the dive boat, the RV *Dragon Lady*, and as soon as we were all on board we were chugging out of the harbor for our first dive. We were all exhausted. The sea was not calm, and *everybody* on board, save one person, got seasick. I was not that one person.

I gathered up my dive gear, put on my mask, stuck the regulator in my mouth, and rolled off the diving platform into the water. I sank to the bottom — about 30 feet down — and just lay there for half an hour. The water was still down there, so I reveled in the lack of motion and calmed my queasy stomach. After that, I donned the rest of my gear and proceeded with the dive, swimming around, exploring coral and tropical fish. It was the first practical use of the "ditch and recovery" technique that I had learned in training.

I wasn't looking forward to surfacing, but eventually had to do so, of course. It took me a day or two to completely gain my sea legs and motion sickness became a thing of the past — to the point that I could sit in the crow's nest 20 feet above the deck and sway back and forth in six-foot seas without a qualm.

We reveled in listening to radio broadcasts from Chicago, where it was close to zero degrees Fahrenheit — as we basked in the tropical sun and dived in 72-degree water.

# Chapter 23

# NASA Co-op Student

## California Here I Come

During my freshman year at the university, I decided to apply for the co-operative (co-op) education program, which would allow me to alternate school with internships in a rotating fashion throughout the year. It would take longer to graduate, but I felt the experience would be worth it. It would also help pay for my college education since these were paid positions. The U of I had a co-op program in place with many organizations in both private industry and government. I applied at 20 different companies and agencies. No bites. It was 1972 and we were in an economic downturn at the end of the Apollo era. Disheartened, I returned home for the summer, jobless. My sister, Theresa, had been very ill and my mother finally convinced me to stay home and help take care of her rather than pounding the bushes looking for a job. My mother had barely convinced me that helping take care of my sister would be productive and useful to her when I got a call from the University. The NASA Flight Research Center at Edwards, CA had accepted me as a co-op student starting in the fall! I was elated. Of all the applications, only one had accepted me — and it was NASA! Since the program would put me at least a year behind in graduation I didn't feel I could afford to take the summer off. So by the next evening I was on the Greyhound bus to Champaign to begin a summer of accelerated courses, which would be starting in a few days.

Then in late August, 1972, I flew to California.

It was the first time I had ever been there. Arriving by air seemed appropriate, given my new job at a flight research center. I caught a connecting flight from Los Angeles to Palmdale and took a taxi to the apartment I had arranged to stay in.

My start date at what was then the NASA Flight Research Center was August 21, 1972 — and my salary as a GS-3 was $5828 per year. In those days, even with that meager starting salary I was nearly able to put myself through college.

So at the age of 19 I was working for NASA! This was the place where legendary flights by legendary pilots took place. A place I had been reading about since the fourth grade. A place where the real was separated from the imagined — and it was the only place out of 20 that had accepted me. I still can't believe my luck.

I had five co-op rotations there over the next four years. For four of them I lived in the same apartment complex with a variety of roommates. The fifth and last rotation I stayed in the new "co-opville" or "Jonestown" — so-called because the landlord's last name was Jones.

When I showed up for work that first day at the Flight Research Center, none of my supervisors were on site. But I was collected by an engineer and deposited in the instrumentation development group — where under one organizational name or another I would spend the next 30 or so years.

At the time I arrived, NASA was still flying Apollo missions to the moon. When I retired, NASA was re-starting deep space exploration activity with Orion flight testing.

## Off-Nominal Testing

One of my earliest jobs at NASA was to design an automatic pressure transducer calibration program. This system would automate the process — which could take up to six hours — of driving temperature chambers and pressure test sets through a pre-determined set of conditions, freeing a technician from the task of monitoring the test and manually driving each test point. As part of the buildup process, I would write "drivers," or hardware-controlling software, for pieces of test equipment and then test them.

Probably the most valuable lesson I learned in that experience was that people often don't know what new technology can do for them until they actually see it work. I would ask the technicians what they wanted the program to do — and they didn't know. They just knew what they did. When I created a program to do what they did manually, they started to see the possibilities and had many suggestions.

When I was working on the programming task for the pressure controller, I wrote a piece of code that would allow an operator to enter pressure values and then watch the pressure controller drive to the set point. I was more proud of this accomplishment than was probably warranted, and invited one of our engineers, Bob Borek, down to take it for a spin. On the teletype unit, he typed in a pressure and watched the test set sail off to the expected value. I beamed. Then he typed in a *negative* number — and the test set didn't know what to do with it. The pressure controller behaved in an unexpected fashion. The "legal" pressures were all positive because they were *absolute* pressures. It didn't know what to do with a negative input.

This was my first exposure to program "robustness" and "off-nominal" testing — testing a program with inputs that are not expected. I learned very quickly to account for illegal conditions and protect the program against them. The next time Bob tested the (revised) program and put in a negative number, the program questioned his intelligence with a snide output.

Knowing Bob, I thought he'd appreciate the humor — and he did.

## The Telephone

As my calibration program matured, it would monitor several pressure transducers while a pressure controller would run them through several pressures and record their outputs. Then the temperature would be changed and another pressure run would be made. It took time for the chamber to stabilize on the next temperature, which would vary from -65 degrees Fahrenheit to +160 degrees Fahrenheit. This is why a six-hour calibration time was not uncommon.

I did not want to sit around and wait for this, so I would return to my office upstairs and periodically check on the progress. One day, I was watching the lights blinking on the computer and my eyes were drawn to the relay register banana plugs on the front panel. Hmmm ... The computer can control the relays ... and the telephone is controlled by a series of switch contact closures ... Hmmm .... So I opened up the lab's dial telephone and reverse-engineered it to see how it worked. Then I hooked up the relay register outputs of the computer to the telephone and wrote a program to control the relays to take the phone off hook, "dial" my extension upstairs, and then ring the bell on the teletype (Morse Code for "done") several times and then hang up.

Now this whole system was hay-wired together — a prototype. So I designed up a box that would make this a more permanent (and reliable) system but ran out of time before the weekend. So I balanced the phone receiver on the hook of the open telephone and went home.

Monday morning I returned to work and got a call from my division chief to come down to his office. When I got there I found the security chief, George Blackwell, sitting there with his arms crossed and a sour expression on his face. Not good. He proceeded to chew me out because I had tampered with a government phone.

"Don't you know that's illegal!?" he barked.

He verbally chased me up one wall and down the other. I was terrified. I left the office shaking. What had I done? Had I torpedoed my career before it got started?

What had happened was this: when the telephone technicians arrived Monday morning, they saw an indication that a phone relay was overheating. In those days this was a normal symptom of a phone being left off-hook for a long period of time. Since security guards had keys to the lab, they were sent down to put the phone back on hook. They entered and saw this phone (the receiver had indeed fallen off hook) with wires coming out everywhere and assumed the worst. This was shortly after the Watergate scandal broke and tapping of phones was in the forefront of everyone's minds.

A few years later, at the end of my last co-op work tour at NASA, I received a greeting card. It read "It had to be you," (turn page) "everyone else had an alibi" — signed, George Blackwell. I was told that George actually thought what I did was clever and didn't take it quite as seriously as he let on when he chewed me out.

## The Musical Computer

In the early days before personal computers existed, mini-computers were expensive and esoteric. One of my first jobs was to upgrade a Hewlett Packard (HP) 2116B minicomputer from 16 kilobytes to 32 kilobytes of memory. The memory was magnetic core — which was hand-woven and not cheap. It turned out that it cost the same to upgrade the memory as it did to buy the next generation minicomputer with 32 kilobytes already installed — $32,000! So we bought the HP 21MX to replace the 2116B. The way to load programs on those computers was through a paper tape reader. We had a "high speed" photoreader that read the tape much faster than the teletype mechanical reader. Even so, the process was labor intensive and subject to frequent loading failures due to the paper tape tearing. In order to compile, load, and run a one-page FORTRAN program, it took about 20 minutes and several paper-tape loadings. Source code, compiler, libraries, and linker/loaders were all on different (long) paper tapes.

Someone had discovered that by sending a series of set control/clear control pulses to the photoreader solenoid you could oscillate it at audio frequencies, and by placing a piece of paper tape crosswise in the unit it acted as a diaphragm and presto — you had a speaker. There were some "absolute" (stand-alone) programs floating around that allowed you to play music by this method. Being a student with nothing better to do on weekends (OK, I was boring), I applied my music background (I played the violin) and my programming background to create a music language that allowed me to enter a piece of sheet music into a source file and compile it into music that could be played on the photoreader. This system achieved some fame locally with other students. I showed one of them how to play it. Unfortunately, he brought some guests in one day and proceeded to demonstrate the music playing — interrupting a multi-hour calibration run that it was doing at the time.

Lab access policy changed after that.

**NASA Career Decision**

Upon graduation in 1976, I was offered the unbelievable chance to start my career in earnest as an electronics engineer

144

at the NASA Dryden Flight Research Center, which had been renamed just months before to honor Dr. Hugh L. Dryden — an enormously influential figure in aeronautical research history. Being the analytic type, and having been offered at least three other jobs that paid more and were in more desirable areas, I thought hard about what my move should be. I even went so far as to call my mother for advice. After she recovered from the shock of that novelty, she asked me one question: "What do you want to be doing for the next five years?"

My answer was immediate and obvious — work at Dryden. My fate was sealed. I had been trying to determine my whole career in one decision. In fact I was, as it turned out, but that wasn't the decision before me. Where did my heart lead me? It led me to NASA.

After graduation, I arrived with one small U-haul trailer toting all my worldly goods, propelled 1,800 miles by my '66 Plymouth Valiant, a car that promptly died the moment I pulled into a friend's driveway in Lancaster, California. I was thankful that Don Bennett, an engineer in my office, had offered to let me stay with him, giving me a chance to look for housing. I am by nature a pack rat, but Don's house was a masterpiece of clutter. That helped motivate me to find my own place as soon as possible.

The first thing I had to do was to take out a loan. My funds were down to near-zero; I used the last of them to make the trip out. My moving costs would be reimbursed, but I wouldn't see that money for two or three weeks — or a paycheck either — and I had rental deposits to make and food to eat in the meantime.

At least I was arriving without debt. Between my co-op work assignments, from which I was able to save about half my pay for each next semester's tuition, and my job at the

University as a lab technician, I had mostly paid my own way through school. My last two semesters at school were back-to-back, however, and that had depleted my funds. I lacked about $1,000, which my parents were able to contribute to the cause.

After I fixed my car, which had a weak coil that wasn't producing enough voltage to create decent sparks in the spark plugs, I moved into my new, rented house on the 4th of July, 1976 — the country's bicentennial. All of my worldly goods fit against one wall of my one-car garage. My life, I felt, was set. My career goal achieved, I set out to immerse myself in my new — yet familiar — job.

# Chapter 24

# Astronaut?

In 1978, the Space Shuttle was coming on-line. NASA prepared for the new Shuttle fleet by opening up applications for a new class of astronauts. It was the first time in nine years that NASA had accepted applications to join the astronaut core. Astronauts had always been pilots — preferably test pilots. Now, NASA had created a new type of astronaut: the mission specialist.

Mission specialists would not be piloting the Space Shuttle. They would be focusing on accomplishing some mission while on orbit. Scientists, engineers, and physicians in particular would be primarily qualified for this new job.

*I* was an engineer. I worked for NASA. I had flight-test experience. I had been trained in SCUBA diving, and I was learning to fly. Hmmm ...

I always dreamed of going into space, but saw no way to make that happen. There was no guaranteed approach for assuring success, but there were things you could do to improve your chances — such as going to graduate school. But I was having too much fun at my job. If I went off to graduate school I would likely come back to a different job, and I was unwilling to rock that boat.

They were only going to select 35 astronaut candidates, and about half of them would be mission specialists. It was a long shot — a *very* long shot — but I knew that I had to try. As my son Sam puts it, "There is 100% chance that I won't be selected if I don't try."

I applied to be a NASA astronaut — along with 8,000 other applicants.

Surprise! I wasn't selected. I didn't even make it to the cut where they called to talk to you or schedule an interview. I have always been curious about how far I made it. Was the application culled out immediately? Did I make it to the last 4,000? Was I still being considered as one of the last several hundred? There was no way to know.

Twice more, in later years, I would apply when astronaut calls were made. Twice more, nothing returned but the rejection letter. Oh well. I was confident NASA would select the best candidates — and that was the big picture. I wanted the space program to be successful. I would devote my energies to doing the best job I could for the agency in my assigned areas — and have fun doing it.

## Skydiving

Part of my thinking was *gee, wouldn't this be good for astronaut training.* Part of it was seizing an opportunity. Part may have been peer pressure; one of my co-op students talked me into going skydiving with them.

In any case, I found myself at a skydiving training class in California City, learning body position, landing technique, and parachuting protocol. It was a minimal class — one weekend — and as subsequent events transpired, I felt I was inadequately prepared for jumping.

When it came time for my first jump, five of us piled into a Cessna 182. The plane was flown by a pilot who just hours before I had witnessed jump with a parachute that had a total malfunction — a streamer. He pulled his reserve chute and landed safely.

I was first up, and on command I checked my static line, climbed out onto the right tire — holding onto the wing strut. A door had been removed to facilitate this. I felt strangely calm.

When given the signal, I lifted my feet, pushed off, and arched my back. What followed was an assault on my senses of things changing rapidly: engine sound disappearing, sense of orientation lost, my arm brushing against the static line. My senses couldn't keep up with the rapid changes. I couldn't take it all in.

Then there was the snap of the parachute opening as the static line reached its maximum length — and a sense of euphoria that the chute had opened. I started bouncing up and down in my harness, grinning from ear to ear. *I had survived*!

Wait — it wasn't over. I still had to land.

As I approached the ground, I looked straight ahead and focused on dropping into a roll when my feet hit the ground, in order to absorb the shock. I landed hard, but pulled off the roll and gathered my chute.

Then I thought about what I had just done. I was struck by the calmness and deliberateness of my climbing out of the plane and jumping — without hesitation. That actually scared me more than the act of jumping. How could I do something like that without apparent thought?

The next weekend I made my second jump. With somewhat more reluctance I showed up and repeated the performance. This time, I took in more of the experience. I saw the plane fall away and heard the plane engine sound disappear — in a better context. I saw the static line extend as I felt it brush against my extended arm.

Once the chute opened, I also saw that the parachute lines had crossed; they were twisted. I had not been trained for that, but I knew it wasn't good. Instinctively, I reached up, grabbed the lines, and gave myself a push to try to spin myself. It worked. The lines untwisted and my chute deployed fully.

A little disconcerted, I approached the ground — and looked down. Bad move. I thought *Gee, the ground is coming up awfully fast,* and it screwed up my timing. I hit the ground — hard again — and started to twist in a belated attempt to initiate the roll. But I didn't fall to the side, I continued straight down, twisting in a vertical position. I felt something snap in my back.

I lay on the ground, the wind knocked out of me. Moving was difficult — stiff. But I got up and recovered, thinking that this was stupid. Why am I doing this? If the chute opens and I land OK, I've got what I started with: my life. If things go wrong, then I could lose everything. Didn't seem like a good use of my time. I don't need an adrenaline rush to feel alive.

However, I actually did make a third jump to wipe out the bad taste of the second. Every time I had closed my eyes I could mentally see the ground rushing up to meet me. The third jump went off without incident, but I was done. The "ground rushing" vision was gone. I had gotten back on the horse, but saw no reason to continue. To further compound things, I was subsequently told by another jumpmaster that the parachute they gave me was too small for someone my size — which causes a harder landing. Also, two of the five people that were in the plane on my first jump had subsequently died in skydiving accidents.

*Maybe I should stay in the plane and learn how to fly it,* I thought.

Six months later, I was painting my house, and was constantly moving my back up and down as I put more paint on the brush. The next morning I awoke feeling like my left leg was on fire; even crawling to the bathroom took me 10 minutes. It was excruciating.

Subsequent examination by an orthopedic surgeon revealed that I had ruptured a disk in my spine, and the ruptured material was putting pressure on my sciatic nerve. I needed surgery to correct it. I had endured the pain for two weeks before the problem was diagnosed.

The doctor told me he needed me to undergo a myelogram — a procedure where they remove some fluid from your spine and then replace it with some dye in order to X-ray it — to verify where the damage was. My mother had two back surgeries when I was very young — and some of my earliest memories were seeing Mommy wrapped up like a mummy lying in a hospital bed. The stories she told of how painful the myelogram was now came to haunt me. When I got up from the doctor's examination table, there was a pool of sweat where I had lain. The doctor looked at that, then me, and said, "You're a little apprehensive about this, aren't you?"

I was single, lived alone, my family was 2,000 miles away — and my only sister was getting married in Missouri the following week. I needed to call my family. How to do that without freaking them out?

"Mom," I said on the phone, "First of all the good news is that I'm OK, but the bad news is I am in the hospital and I'm going to need back surgery."

I had asked the doctor if there was any way I could make it to that wedding. He stroked his chin and said, "If we do the myelogram tomorrow and confirm what I'm sure we'll see, do the surgery the following day, and get you out of bed the day after that, we should be able to get you on a plane a couple of days after that — if you fly first class."

And that's what happened. I even ushered at Theresa's wedding.

My surgery was successful. Surgical techniques had improved a great deal in the intervening 20 years since my mother's back surgeries, and my convalescence was considerably shorter than hers. Even the myelogram turned out to be painless.

I never was sure if I should tell people that I ruptured a disk painting my house, which was ridiculous, or by parachuting — which was stupid. The reality was that the parachute landing did the damage, and the painting made it worse.

This entire episode knocked me out of work for six weeks. By the end of three, I felt ready to return, but the doctor wouldn't authorize it. Being 25 years old, I bounced back pretty quickly. So I spent my time standing up in my garage building a microcomputer system that I had designed. It was 1978, and it was shortly after the Apple II personal computer debuted. My system and the Apple II had similar capabilities, but Job's genius marketed Wosniak's brilliantly elegant creation to great success. My system remained a single unit built as a hobby.

## Learning to Fly

Working at the NASA Dryden Flight Research Center, flying was at the center of all activity. Any design I that worked on, any hardware that I built, was ultimately to support flight research. My brother, Joe, had learned to fly. I grew up next to an international airport and McDonnell fighters flew over my house frequently.

It seemed that my life had put me on a flying trajectory. I needed to learn to fly.

The town of Rosamond, California had a small airport, and a retired USAF test pilot, Walt Schob, was starting a flying school there through the local fixed-based operator, Arsonson's Air Service. Rosamond Airport was a classic small airport with no control tower and sparse population surrounding it — and was about 15 miles from where I lived in Lancaster. There was no formal ground school, but as an engineer, picking up the basics wasn't difficult.

I flew a Piper Tomahawk nearly every day for three weeks, and one day after I had executed seven takeoffs and landings; Walt stepped out of the cockpit, said "Take 'er up," and closed the door.

Taking a deep breath, I fired up the engine again, taxied out to runway 26 and rolled. I lifted off, flew once around the pattern, and then set it back down on the runway.

Having survived that milestone, Walt wrote in my logbook: "Glenn Bever did defy the laws of gravity and solo on this day!" We then went back to the office, where he cut out the back of my T-shirt, wrote my name and date on it, and tacked it to the wall — where it joined other T-shirt backs with similar inscriptions.

A student pilot is required to log time with a number of different types of flying: including cross-country, solo flight, instructed flight, and night flight. For my night flight, Walt had a friend of his, who was an active USAF Test Pilot School instructor, come out and run me through the paces. I flew to Van Nuys Airport — which was one of the busiest small airports in the country and also sat in the busy Los Angeles airspace — and did take offs and landings, or "touch-and-goes." A *lot* of touch-and-goes. After about 20 of them, he reached over and shut off the lights of my instrument panel and said, "Now land it."

*What?* I thought. *But I can't see my instruments!*

*Use the force, Luke. Stretch out with your feelings.*

So I discovered that by using the lights of the city as references, listening to the pitch of the engine, and feeling the response of the aircraft; I could, in fact, land the airplane. While you learn to trust your instruments, you also learn to trust the sensors in your body. This is important in emergencies. Flying by the seat of your pants is a literal feel of the aircraft situation as sensed by your body. Guess which part of your body is most attached to the aircraft.

A few years later I was flying into Mojave airport at night, on low final approach, when suddenly all the airport lights went out. I had suddenly lost all my ground reference points. I instantly realized what had happened, grabbed my radio microphone and started clicking the push-to-talk switch like mad. The airport lights came back on and I completed my landing successfully.

The airport lights were on a timer, activated by pilots landing there. What had happened was that I was landing on another pilot's "nickel" and the time had run out. It was like using the time left on a parking meter fed by somebody else.

It's easy to forget details, but you have to apply reason, training, and experience-based instinct to survive. Nothing beats not getting *into* dicey situations though. There is a saying attributed to Astronaut Frank Borman:

"A superior pilot uses his superior judgment to avoid situations which require the use of his superior skill."

After four months I had accumulated enough hours and demonstrated enough proficiency to go for a check ride with an

FAA examiner, and after he signed off that I had satisfactorily completed the requirements for a private pilot's license, he turned to me and said, "You now have a license to learn."

I have remembered those words often when I learn something new. Don't get cocky, there is *always* something to learn.

# Chapter 25

# Projects that I Worked On

Over the course of my career with NASA, I worked on 17 aircraft involved in flight research projects. A few of the more memorable ones I discuss in this chapter. The discussion is, of necessity, more technical, since that was the nature of the work I was doing.[1]

## STS-1 Decom

Shortly before the Space Shuttle, also known as the Space Transportation System (STS) first flew into space in 1981, one of our top aeronautics researchers, Dr. Ken Iliff, became interested in collecting data from the shuttle during reentry. It was a unique opportunity to gather atmospheric flight data at Mach 25! However, the format of the data stream from the shuttle was peculiar. It had three embedded data streams in the main data stream that were non-standard, and our range group at Dryden did not have a way of cracking out the data Ken wanted in real time. I happened to be in a meeting where this was being discussed one day and made the observation that I thought I knew a way to do it. I instantly got the job of making it happen!

I had been working with some equipment that I repurposed for this activity. The process would involve decommutating the main data stream (pulling out individual words from a serial frame and stuffing them into known memory locations), then re-stringing them together to form a new telemetry stream buffered through a first-in-first-out (FIFO) memory, and then

---

[1]  Refer to the glossary for further explanation of some of the terms.

156

metering them out at a new telemetry rate. Or, more simply put, I disassembled the data stream and rebuilt it into three new data streams that the range could process using standard means. I successfully demonstrated the ability to do this using a magnetic tape unit loaded with a tape of data from a simulated shuttle mission — reading off data from one tape track and writing back to other tracks.

The plan was to drop a coaxial cable outside from the third floor range receivers down to my lab on the first floor, perform the magic; then run other coaxes back up to the third floor to input into their decommutators. However, a month before the shuttle was to fly my equipment broke and I was scheduled to go on a one-month vacation to the South Pacific I had already paid for. Fortunately, the range group figured out their own solution and no longer required my system in order to get the shuttle data. So I went on my vacation (the one where I met Buzz Aldrin) and Dr. Iliff got his data. He privately credited me with making it possible — because he felt that the range group would not have made the effort to come up with a solution if I had not demonstrated that it were possible.

## KC-135 Winglet Flight Project

In 1980 I got involved with the KC-135 Winglet flight project. Its mission was to examine the viability of winglets — upswept wingtips — in reducing aircraft fuel consumption. It was a quantitative study involving instrumentation to measure fuel flow. I did not design the instrumentation system; however I had some data acquisition equipment that I wanted to test — and the KC-135 represented a platform that would allow me to test it. The existing system was passive in the sense that it collected data and telemetered it but did no computations. As I mentioned earlier, I went to the project manager, Russ Barber, and asked if he would allow my equipment to be put on board. He acquiesced on the condition that it would not interfere with the mission and could be rapidly restored to the original configuration if problems arose. I agreed.

The data acquisition system was a controlled by a Remote Multiplexer Digitizer Unit (RMDU) that sequenced the sampling of sensors. I slotted in a master/slave data acquisition controller — or RMDU Controller Unit (RCU) — to allow a master system to control the sequencing instead of the Stand Alone Timing Module (SATM). This permitted me to interface to a PDP-11 mini-computer, giving it access to the data being collected. I had already designed a digital interface card that contained an Intel 8085 microprocessor to replace a discrete logic controller that controlled the fuel flow data acquisition.

I then developed some display software so that I could monitor the data. I demonstrated its utility in some early local flight tests. It worked — and the project began to see some of its possibilities. The aircraft needed to go outside of our range area and fly over the ocean for the bulk of the data collection. My system would allow them to monitor the data on-board when they were out of range and increase the efficiency of the flight test since they could make real-time calls regarding how good the data runs were — and repeat them if necessary while they were still on flight condition. It would also be able to perform a real-time fuel-consumption calculation and totalize it over the flight. Since the aircraft was weighed before and after the flight, the calculated totalization could be compared to the actual aircraft weight change — which would give you the measurement error of the fuel consumption calculations. (The computation was within 200 pounds of the actual measured weight change — which was between 100,000 and 200,000 pounds over a six- or seven-hour mission. It was a tiny error, well under 1%.)

The project data ultimately showed an increase in fuel mileage of 6% to 7%,[2] which led to industry interest in using winglets to improve fuel efficiency on other aircraft. Today, their use is ubiquitous. Every time I see a commercial aircraft fly overhead using winglets, it reminds me that I had a big hand in producing the data that significantly impacted the way aircraft wings are now designed.

So my system became a requirement for the flight program and I became a regular member of the flight crew — charged with monitoring the health of my system and taking corrective action if needed.

Because the system usually functioned normally, I had lots of free time to observe the flight test. I would sit at the console during takeoff and landing and then relinquish the seat to the Boeing flight-test researcher during the data runs. I spent a lot of my time standing between the pilots, watching their operation. There were three principle pilots that flew missions: Fitz Fulton, Tom McMurtry, and Royce Grones. Fitz and Tom were NASA pilots and Royce was Air Force. Rounding out the crew was the navigator, who was always Air Force. Fitz and Tom had entirely different flying styles. Fitz was a former Air Force "heavy" (large airplane) pilot with a ton of experience flying large aircraft of all stripes. When he landed, he greased it onto the runway. You often couldn't tell when you had actually landed. Tom, a former Navy pilot, had a somewhat more aggressive style — being trained to slam an aircraft down on a small carrier deck to catch the wire.

---

[2] *KC-135 Winglet Program Review*, NASA Conference Publication 2211, September 1981

One of my pastimes during the missions was to watch the Air Force navigator — if he was new to the program — when we landed with Tom at the controls. Upon setting up for landing, I would move my seat back on its rails, pivot 90 degrees to face forward, and keep my eye on the navigator. Tom would do a high-bank turn to base leg and final and set it down "firmly." A new navigator would usually react with surprise at the very least. Once, the Edwards commanding general was in the tower and observed one of these unorthodox maneuvers. He got on the radio and called our aircraft to see if something was wrong. Air Force pilots are not used to seeing a Navy-style landing with that large an aircraft.

This particular KC-135 had done service as an astronaut zero-G trainer. Astronauts would be back in the main cabin, which had all the seats stripped out and padding applied to the surfaces, when the aircraft pilot would perform a parabolic arc maneuver. The aircraft would gain altitude and then the pilot would "push over" the nose and free fall over the top of the arc. The astronauts and safety crew in the cabin would then experience zero-G conditions, meaning they were "weightless." They were falling at the same rate as the aircraft around them.

This condition would only last maybe 20 seconds before the pilot had to stop the freefall and return to normal flight. They would then repeat this maneuver multiple times, giving the astronauts time to practice operating in a space-like environment.

For our research flights, we would often execute a maneuver called the "push-over pull-up" — or "po-pu." This was used to test sensor operation, validate equations of motion, and sometimes to help characterize the flying qualities of the aircraft. This maneuver is done all the time in test flights.

Since I often had nothing else to do during the flight, I realized I could take advantage of this maneuver to have a little fun. Following along the flight card, I knew when the po-pu's would be performed. At those times I would unstrap from my seat, get up, move toward the rear of the aircraft, and wait for the call.

"Everyone ready?" Tom would call over the intercom — meaning was everyone strapped in?

"Roger," I would reply, and get down on the floor in a push-up position.

Tom would push forward on the yoke and I would start to do pushups. As the aircraft descended, I got lighter and I would start to do pushups on the tips of one finger. Very quickly Tom would pull back on the yoke and I would revert to normal pushups — which got much harder as we then started to pull positive G's.

"Maneuver complete," Tom would call, and I would return to my seat and strap in.

I was, of course, violating the spirit of Tom's query about readiness for the maneuver. I was supposed to remain securely strapped in my seat for the duration of the po-pu, but knowing the history of the aircraft and the lessor magnitude of the po-pu maneuver, I felt comfortable in pushing the envelope of safety procedure for the sake of entertainment.

I never did cop to my transgression.

During one of my meanderings about the aircraft during a test flight I heard a hissing sound. Since the noise level onboard is very high, hearing a hissing sound was noteworthy. Investigating, I discovered that I could see daylight through the seal surrounding one of the fuselage doors. The hissing was pressurized air in the cabin escaping the aircraft. This alarmed me — remembering the James Bond movie *Goldfinger* where the villain was sucked out of the aircraft through a small opening when an aircraft window broke — so I immediately reported it to the pilot. McMurtry waved it off saying that the aircraft had a robust enough pressure system to overcome a leak like that.

So much for Goldfinger.

Once when we were flying at altitude, about 35,000 feet, the test card called for dropping to 25,000 feet and lowering the landing gear. At that altitude, the pilot pulled the gear levers but the gear did not deploy. This did not bode well for subsequent aircraft landing. Apparently, after cold-soaking at that high altitude for some hours, the hydraulic fluid used to deploy the gear was too thick to perform as needed. Fortunately, the aircraft had a manual system, and we cranked the gear down by hand. Of course, we were all inside the aircraft and couldn't visually check that the hand crank had been successful. The pilots called the issue in and the Air Force sent one of their airborne F-4 *Phantom*s over to check us out. They confirmed a good deployment and we landed without further incident, although the "foam" trucks had been positioned by the runway in preparation of a possible "belly" landing — or worse.

Another incident I remember was during ground testing. Jet aircraft often require a ground starter cart to get the engines cranking. We were onboard going through startup procedures when we heard a large BANG outside. The starter cart engine had quit in a spectacularly loud and smoky fashion. Fortunately nobody was hurt, but it sure got my attention. Considering that the sound level inside the KC-135 with all its engines going was deafening, it was noteworthy that we could even hear the bang.

The crew got another starter cart and we pressed on.

Later in the program I had scheduled leave to join my church group in a volunteer service project in Sitka, Alaska. We went up to act as maintenance and repair crew for Sheldon Jackson College. As we were in the middle of a set of KC-135 research flights, Russ was apprehensive about my approaching absence.

"What if something goes wrong and you're not here to fix it?" he asked.

Frankly, the program wasn't critical enough for them to cancel my leave. That seldom happened at Dryden.

"Would you be willing to come back if we fly an F-104 up to get you?" Russ asked me.

We had some supersonic F-104 *Starfighters* that we used for chase work. A couple of them were two-seaters.

I allowed as how if he did that, then I would gladly return.

So I went on my vacation. Travel to Sitka was a combination of flying to Seattle, taking the Alaska Ferry up the inland passage, stopping at Ketchikan and Juneau, then flying to Sitka where I was to work for a couple of weeks as an electrician. I discovered that electrical building codes meant little in an environment where hardware stores weren't handy. Wires often changed color in the middle of a conduit when they ran out of the right color. Alaskans tend to be fiercely independent and frontiersmen focus more on getting the job done than following rules.

One day I got called to the main office for a phone call. Turns out that Russ had been trying to reach me, but I had not left any contact information. It took him a couple of days to track me down. He told me that my system was having problems and asked me to return to fix it. While I wasn't happy about aborting my vacation, I had enough pride in my work and the mission to agree to come back — although it would not be by F-104. The pilots' office had nixed that idea for logistical reasons. If the fighter broke in Alaska, they didn't have the facilities to fix it. So I boarded a commercial airplane for the flight back.

Now everyone has experienced this: your appliance fails and you call the technician. When they arrive it works perfectly. The same thing happened here. Upon my return I could find nothing wrong with the equipment and it worked perfectly. So it would appear that cutting my leave short was to no avail — but there was an epilogue that made it worthwhile.

One day late in the program, we were cruising along at altitude. I was standing in my customary spot between the two pilots, when Tom McMurtry turned to me and said, "When the project slows down, you and I will go up in an F-104."

I think my earlier statement that flying me back in an F-104 would make aborting my leave worthwhile ended up translating to this proposal. I wasn't going to let that slide by unfulfilled, so every few days over the next month I would stop by the pilots' office and ask when our flight was going to be.

One day, unexpectedly, Tom said "How about now?"

So almost before I knew it, I found myself in one of the tandem seats of an F-104 *Starfighter*, where Tom taught me how to roll the aircraft and let me punch the throttle to Mach 1.6. We had to cut the flight a little short due to the NASA Administrator visiting that day on his farewell tour of NASA centers, but that flight lives on as a personal highlight of my career. My only regret is that it happened so fast I had no chance to have any pictures taken of the event. But it is indelibly etched in my memory.

## F-15 DEEC

The first aircraft to demonstrate an electronic engine controller was an F-15 flown at NASA Dryden. The project was called DEEC, for Digital Electronic Engine Control. It was a bit of a hodge-podge system that required various custom interfaces. One interface that didn't exist was one from the DEEC to the RMDU data acquisition system. I had been thinking about developing a microprocessor-based unit to display airspeed and altitude information to an F-104 pilot for airspeed calibration work, so I designed a system that would do that as well as interface to the F-15 DEEC. DEEC was the first application for that system. I designed a microprocessor board which was the first multi-layer printed circuit board (PCB) designed at Dryden and I had it manufactured at the Navy facility at China Lake. However, before I had printed circuit boards fabricated, I "breadboarded" (prototyped) it using wire-wrap — but I used cards that were the same physical form factor as the PCBs would be. I also had an enclosure built that would accommodate either the PCBs or the wire-wrap boards, which allowed me to test the design on the aircraft and then slot in the manufactured PCBs later.

When I had successfully demonstrated the design using the breadboards, the project manager, anxious to fly, said "let's test it in flight." I wasn't sanguine about that. The system had not been environmentally tested. Wire-wrap boards had long pins that would be more sensitive to vibration. But we "gooped up" sections of the PCBs to keep parts from shaking off — and flew. I bit my nails as the aircraft exceeded Mach one and performed engine stalls. But it worked! After this flight, I moved quickly to get PCBs made that were better suited to reliably work in the flight environment.

**Army OV-1 Stall Speed Warning**

The U.S. Army had a facility on the Edwards flight line called the Army Aviation Engineering Flight Activity

165

(AAEFA). The Army OV-1 *Mohawk* had a particularly nasty stall characteristic. An aircraft stall is a point, usually with the nose too high, that it stops flying and starts to fall out of the sky. An aircraft typically gives warning signs to the pilot — it flies too mushy, it shudders, the controls don't respond right, or something. When a pilot senses approaching stall, he/she can take corrective action. However, the OV-1 would stall upon landing without any warning. It was killing pilots.

NASA Ames Research Center (of which Dryden was a part in those days) had a joint project with the Army to demonstrate a stall-speed warning system. The Ames researcher, Jerry Brown, had demonstrated a stall warning system on an Ames transport class aircraft and wanted to translate it to the Army OV-1 using a small contractor company to do the work. As it was easier to get things through the Dryden procurement process than the Ames procurement process, we were asked to write the statement of work to make this happen. I got assigned the task.

The contractor started work — and then went bankrupt. Due to the way the contract was written, the Army took the point of view that NASA had agreed to get the job done and we had to come up with another way to do it. Again, it fell to me. So I designed a system to do it, based on the same unit I used for the DEEC project. It was a very interesting project where I and another Dryden engineer, Doug Wilner, got to design/ buy several interfaces, including EEPROM, digital-to-analog converters, synchro-to-DC converters, and even a voice synthesizer to give aural feedback to the pilot. It was pretty crude, but voice synthesizers were brand new and I built one based on the SC-01 phoneme synthesizer.

Professor Art Hoadley and I wrote all the software — in assembly language — to control the system. Art was also able to program in an algorithm that he developed that he called the "stall margin indicator." It would compute stall speed at any flight condition — which we were already doing — but then it would display the current airspeed as a percent above the current stall speed. This was the stall margin. So regardless of the current stall speed (which changed with the angle of attack, flap settings, even engine rotation speed), you would have a consistent indication of how close you were to stall by referencing the display indicating your percentage above stall speed, rather than having to add airspeed based on mental computations or guesses accounting for the current aircraft flight condition.

This is an example of squeezing some flight research out of a program with operational requirements.

It was a fun project — made even more fun when the Army allowed me to fly in a T-28 chasing the OV-1. As I had my pilot's license by then, the Army pilot let me fly it sometimes.

One day, I was fighting the beginnings of a cold, but was still — I judged — able to fly.

Strike one.

The T-28 engine exhaust seems to be directed right through the cockpit.

Strike two.

So we are flying along, me in the rear cockpit, the pilot in the front — and he hands the aircraft off to me. I was flying on the OV-1 wing in extended formation when the combination of exhaust and infirmity led to an all too familiar sensation; I was getting airsick.

Before I could take any action, I started to barf.

Strike three.

Now I was still flying in formation. I couldn't choke any words out to tell the pilot to take control of the aircraft. Pilot rule number one: fly the aircraft. I had no option but to barf in a bag that I had at the ready and also keep the aircraft flying steady with near zero tolerance for error. Finally I was able to choke out "take the aircraft" and I could relax — and discretely hide evidence of my weakness in my flight suit pocket.

## AICS

The heart of the system that I built for the F-15 DEEC system, the OV-1 system, as well as several other aircraft, initially had no name. It had become known to project team members as the "Bever Box" — after my last name. (My name rhymes with "fever.") One day my boss, Earl Wilson, called me into his office and suggested that the name "Bever Box" was not very dignified and I should come up with another name. So I started the game that NASA has become famous for — dreaming up an acronym, or at least a pronounceable abbreviation. I settled on the name "Airborne Instrumentation Computer System" (AICS)[3] and that name stuck.

I had made a full set of mechanical drawings for the enclosure to house the processor card and the input/output cards that interfaced it to telemetry, data acquisition systems, and data storage. I then had our shop construct it from parts fabricated in our machine shop.

I was proud of this effort and was pleased with the resulting box. So I asked the shop to build another. When I received that box I noted there were subtle differences between that box and the first one.

---

[3] *The Development of an Airborne Instrumentation Computer System for Flight Test,* by Bever, NASA TM-86036, April 1984

The technician, Wes Hughes, told me "Oh, the parts as designed didn't work quite right so I jiggered the parts to make them fit."

Our technicians had the "can do" spirit and were proud of "fixing" the engineers' designs. Of course, not *telling* the engineers that there was a problem did not give us the opportunity to fix the design so that jiggering would not be required the next time. The fact that the jiggering was different each time was also unfortunate. Most of the things we built at Dryden were one-of-a-kind, so the consistency issue was typically not a big one — but it made it more difficult to swap parts if you built other systems that were ostensibly the same design.

## AIMS

By now well versed in the acronym game, when I started developing a new, much more powerful system than the AICS, I settled on a name early on — The Airborne Information Management System (AIMS). Key features were to be: modularity, operation in harsh environments, distributability (computational nodes distributed around the aircraft), and high processing power. We decided to explore a fluid-filled system to allow it to operate in high temperature environments such as an engine compartment or high altitude where heat transfer via thinner air is a problem.

While I was the principal architect, we formed a fairly ad-hoc team to take on different aspects of the design. In those days, NASA did not keep close accounting of how employees' time was used. You didn't necessarily have to account for development activity by assigning it to an active, funded project. This gave us a lot of flexibility in doing research and development that did not give a project manager an immediate payoff. We also had money for university grants, and contracted with two professors to develop different aspects of this new system. Professor Art Hoadley of Western Michigan University looked into the thermodynamics of a fluid-filled system and came up with techniques to manage it. Professor Alan Hale of Eastern Washington University "took point" on looking at the field of processors available at the time and he settled on the Inmos Transputer, which had some interesting and unique features useful for what we had in mind: intrinsic parallel processing, a unique computer language (OCCAM) to take advantage of that, simple high-speed serial links to network Transputers together (and support their distribution), and minimal components required to support its operation.

I took the lead in designing the processor board and telemetry interface. Terry Montgomery designed the MIL-STD-1553 interface. Dave Wagner led the power-supply interface design and printed circuit board layouts as well as the mechanical design of the enclosure modules.[4]

Due to the lack of hard schedule and communication issues (this was slightly before email became routine) it took a while to develop this system. Its first implementation was on the F-15 ACTIVE program — where we put three AIMS systems that flew for about 15 years — and was also the last AIMS to be decommissioned in 2009 when NASA #837 made its last flight with Jim Smolka at the controls. Other NASA aircraft that utilized an AIMS included the SR-71, F-18, and F-16XL. This system was my most significant design effort, and never had a component failure in operation.

---

[4] *The Development of an Airborne Information Management System for Flight Test*, by Bever, NASA TM-104251, September 1992

## The Tour

When I was a young engineer, I worked on a system called the Airborne Integrated Flight Test Data System (AIFTDS). The RMDU was part of this system. One day, the NASA administrator was touring Dryden and the lab I worked in was on the itinerary. I was supposed to stand behind the computer and at the proper moment throw a switch to activate a printout of the demo test in progress. Everything was checked out and tested. So I waited, in position, for the tour to show up. The entourage entered the back door and the engineer conducting this part of the tour went into his spiel. At the proper moment, I threw the switch and ... nothing. No printout.

I tried again. No response.

After some awkward moments, the tour guide said, "Well, it was *supposed* to print out the results."

Then the tour moved on and out the front door of the lab. Moments after they departed the printer started printing! I felt like running out and yelling "Come back! Come back! It's working!" but I knew that it would have been anti-climactic.

## ATLAS

Although the flying characteristics of different types of aircraft vary, the flight controls themselves are similar. All planes have a throttle to control power. All have either a yoke or stick to control pitch and roll. Most have rudders to control yaw. Some have brakes. But an SR-71 flies quite differently from a Cessna 152. Their design points are quite different. Their speed and altitude capabilities (flight envelope) are also very different.

When a new aircraft is designed and built, it has to be tested to make sure its flight characteristics are well understood and documented. When pilots train to fly a particular aircraft type, this documentation, in the form of a flight manual, is their "bible." They rely on it to tell them how fast and high they can go, how slow they can go and at what attitude, how much runway they need to take off at what atmospheric conditions, etc. So it is very important that the flight manual be right.

Test pilots are the pilots who gather this information by flying the aircraft for the first time, when there are a lot of things that are not well understood about how the aircraft flies. The flight manual is rudimentary at that point and is based on simulations, calculations, and data from previous similar aircraft — if there are any.

In order to assess the characteristics of how an aircraft behaves when controlled by a pilot, its handling qualities are assessed by the test pilot. As every pilot is different, their opinions of how an aircraft behaves — or ought to behave — often differ as well. I saw that amplified by listening to Russian and American pilots talking about how the F-18 versus the Tu-144 handled. It was obvious they were using different yardsticks.

So several test pilots will fly an aircraft and evaluate its handling qualities based, in part, on a set of criteria called Cooper-Harper ratings. This is an attempt to "decouple" the pilot's subjectivity from the process by giving him/her a series of tasks that are not typically done in normal flying. It takes the ego out and puts rating numbers in. Several pilots' ratings are totted up and an assessment of whether an aircraft is, for example, too sensitive or too sluggish for a given task is evaluated.

Flight control designers are interested in this evaluation because it helps them improve aircraft control system designs. Researchers will devise new testing strategies in order to get evaluations that improve their ability to design control systems.

In the late 1980s, one of our handling qualities research engineers, Mary Shafer, asked me to design a ground array that would randomly turn on targets (lights) to help test pilots evaluate an air-to-ground handling qualities task.[5] She was working this task in conjunction with students in the U.S. Air Force Test Pilot School at Edwards.

It was a fun project. My small team and I cobbled together pieces meant for different purposes, and I designed some new pieces using a combination of radio-controlled model aircraft hardware and microprocessors to allow each light to be controlled in a pseudo-random sequence. Each station had a gasoline generator to power it and the station lights were controlled by a master unit, whose sequences were initiated by a pilot in the air via a radio signal. When deployed in the desert to support a flight test, we ran around making sure the generators were still running and rabbits hadn't chewed the wires. The ground lighting array system was officially dubbed the Adaptable Target Lighting Array System (ATLAS) — or as we informally referred to it, the FLID (Flashlights in Desert).

Since the X-29A project was a joint venture with the German research organization DLR, their pilots also flew it. We invited some of the German team to deploy with us in the desert during a flight, and they joined us.

Bouncing over the dirt roads to the site of the lighting array, we set up a tent awning for shade and plopped down a cooler full of water and ice that Mary had brought. It was going to be a hot day and, as always in the Mojave Desert, dry.

---

[5] *Initial Flight Test of a Ground Deployed System for Flying Qualities Assessment*, by Shafer, Koehler, Wilson, and Levy, NASA TM 101700, August 1989

We invited the Germans to have some water, but one responded, "We're Germans, we don't drink water — only beer."

"You don't understand," Mary told them, "The dry air will suck the moisture out of you and you won't notice it. You have to drink water."

They still demurred. I heard later that one of them ended up at the hospital with dehydration.

The pilot's task when flying on the ATLAS was to point the aircraft "pipper," or targeting icon on his heads-up display, at whichever ATLAS light was on — and then evaluate how the aircraft responded to the task. A TF-104G, X-29A, and Calspan NT-33A were among the aircraft that flew against this array.

I was given the opportunity to try it myself. It is helpful to me to experience what a user of my system does; so I strapped into the Calspan NT-33A, which was a variable stability jet aircraft that had been modified to be an airborne simulator. It had the capability to "pretend" to be different aircraft by electronically altering how the aircraft control surfaces responded to a pilot's inputs. For my flight, it was configured to fly like an F-16 fighter.

On the day of my flight, the heads-up display (HUD) failed, so after a fruitless effort to fix it while we sat sweating in the cockpit, we decided to go anyway. My targeting would be done more crudely — aiming a protruding airdata probe near the nose at the ground targets.

We took off and the instructor pilot (IP) demonstrated some maneuvers and then let me handle the aircraft. When I was ready, we flew over to the ATLAS area. The instructor pilot lined up on the targets and then handed control over to me. I initiated the sequence by clicking the microphone several times and then squinted to pick out what lights were on. It was like a video game, only I was aiming a real aircraft at targets as they came to bear.

We capped off the flight by shooting some "touch-and-goes," or landing/takeoff combinations, back on the main Edwards runway. As I was a licensed pilot (and in fact had been trained by test pilots), the instructor pilot let me attempt a landing. Not being rated in either the T-33 or the F-16, which was being simulated, he "flew close" as I lined up and began my approach, his hands hovering close to the controls in the cockpit behind me. To further complicate things, I was using a side stick to control aircraft attitude rather than a center stick. I had never flown with a side stick before, but I found its feel to be quite natural.

So I imagine the IP's "pucker factor" was high as this un-rated pilot brought the aircraft in. I was on glide slope and just starting to flare as the aircraft neared touchdown, when suddenly all my controls went limp! All tension on the stick and rudders disappeared, and I realized that I no longer had control of the aircraft. My control stick flopped around loosely as I vainly tried to make the aircraft respond to my inputs.

There was no time to panic, but there was no time to take any action either as we were moments away from contacting the ground.

Alarmed, I was opening my mouth to call to the IP that I had lost control, when I heard him say, "Oops. I dumped you. I was premature; your landing looked good."

He had hit the switch to transfer control from me to him. The aircraft was under his control and the system was designed to release all tension on my control inputs when I was not commanding the aircraft flight. I didn't realize that, so I had an anxious few moments when I thought that *nobody* was in control.

That fraction of a second was a long time in pilot years.

He returned control to me after applying power to gain altitude. We went around the pattern and this time he did not interfere as I took it in to a solid landing.

# Chapter 26

# Concorde

May, 2000

I was excited. I was on my way to New York to fly in the Concorde, the world's only commercial supersonic jet airplane. I had traveled to Moscow 19 times over a four-year period and accumulated a large number of frequent flyer miles — all on Delta Airlines. I discovered that Delta partnered with Air France and that I could use Delta miles for Air France Concorde flights. I had built up enough miles for a round trip across the Atlantic, and I had a meeting to go to in France. Perfect!

Well, almost perfect. I had gotten married the previous month and my new wife, Irene, was going with me to France — but I only had enough frequent flyer miles for one. Not wanting to disappoint me, Irene agreed to let me take the Concorde flights while she flew coach on normal, subsonic aircraft.

Concordes only flew to France from New York. They were so loud that they were restricted in what areas they could overfly. So I flew in normal commercial aircraft from Los Angeles to New York and spent the night there so that I could catch the Concorde flight the following morning. After a good, but excited, night's sleep, I went to the airport's Concorde lounge, where I found an opulently appointed, first-class area filled with food and comfortable chairs. While waiting there I heard the very loud arrival of the Concorde and rushed to a window to glimpse it.

When it finally came time to board the aircraft, I was struck by how narrow the isle and seats were. I was seated in an aisle seat, which gave my long legs a bit more freedom to move.

The flight itself was an experience. There was a Mach meter in the front of the cabin so the passengers could track the aircraft speed. It was a thrill to see the number change to 2.0 — Mach 2! At one point during Mach flight, a flight attendant came back and offered to let me see the cockpit. So I grabbed my video camera and spent quite some time videotaping flight operations in the cockpit, feeling the heat on the overhead bulkhead, and seeing the effects of airframe stretching due to that heat — which is caused by friction at supersonic speeds. I also had filmed the takeoff, which was very loud. I could understand why the cabin noise experiment on the Tu-144 was of interest.

As we landed in Paris, I realized that my connecting flight to Marseilles was a short turn and I was apprehensive about making it across the airport and through passport control in time. So I asked a flight attendant about it and she said, "No problem. When you exit the aircraft, you will see two people at the bottom of the stairs. Tell them your problem and they will take care of you."

They did. They immediately took me to a crew van and accompanied me across the airport, took me to the front of the line and saw me ensconced in the gate area for my next flight — all within 20 minutes of the time wheels touched down in the Concorde! So this is how the wealthy live.

Landing in Marseilles, I now had to wait for Irene's flight. I spotted her trudging across the airport with luggage in tow and I bounded over to greet her. I was so full of my adventure stories on the Concorde that I failed to notice that she was about done in. "I have been flying all night in coach and am worn out" she said, sleepily. "I really don't want to hear about your first class experience just now."

Oops.

I had a lot to learn. Eighteen years later, I am still learning. Sustaining personal relationships has been harder for me than learning Russian.

After the meetings were over, we again flew back separately. It was a bit surreal arriving back in New York *before* I took off in Paris. I had outrun the time zones.

Two months later, the Air France Concorde crashed on takeoff from Paris, killing all on board. It was the beginning of the end of the Concorde era. I had taken one of the last flights.

# Chapter 27

# Looking Back

It seems like yesterday that I was a wet-behind-the-ears college student arriving for my first work period at NASA. Since then I have done a lot of interesting things and been around a lot of unique aircraft and people. I was trained to fly by test pilots. I've flown supersonic jet aircraft; met astronauts and celebrities; traveled overseas scores of times; been deployed in Russia in the wild and woolly days after the Soviet Union broke up; designed, built, tested, and operated my own computer creations; worked on 17 different research aircraft; led two NASA branch organizations; and helped to lead a directorate — even acting for a time as the directorate head. I have met foreign dignitaries; "starred" in a German documentary; and have witnessed much history being made, like the first landing of the Space Shuttle and the landing of the *Voyager* on its record non-stop round the world flight. I hold all these experiences in my heart. Just a regular guy that got to sample a number of experiences.

Somehow the 42 years flew by and I find myself at the other end, looking back. I can't imagine a better career. I loved doing design work and spent many happy hours solving problems and dreaming up new designs. The travel I did was completely unexpected. In fact, most of my career was unplanned. I just took advantage of opportunities as they came up. Working for NASA, there were many opportunities.

My Russian experience was the most unusual. I got to meet and work with talented engineers in an environment I never imagined would be possible. Throughout most of my career, any thought I gave to the Cold War was in the background. Then the rules changed and Russia was *not* our enemy. We wanted to work together — and we did.

All of my travels have shown me that while cultures differ, people around the world have the same basic desires — to lead a satisfying life in a safe environment for themselves and their families. If you ever have the opportunity to actually get to know people with different backgrounds, cultures, and life experiences, I encourage you to do so. It will enrich your lives far beyond what you might imagine.

# Epilogue

In June of 1999, the Tu-144LL program ended. Tupolev still held out hope that this would just be a lull and American interest in the Tu-144 would rise again. Judith DePaul stood in front of the group at the final shindig in Moscow and adamantly promised that the program would continue. It was, of course, out of her control, but it was a valiant attempt to keep the momentum going.

In a smaller gathering at the Zhukovsky laboratory, we said our goodbyes to the Russian technical team with which we worked closely. On that occasion I decided on the spur of the moment to relax my alcohol prohibition and lifted a glass of vodka in a toast to friendship.

It was a bittersweet moment. It would be my last trip to Russia. It would be the last time I saw any of the Russians that I had worked with on the program. It would be the last time that such a collaboration was even attempted. It wasn't long after that both Russian and American leadership changed, and geopolitical forces in the world shifted once again.

I was gone, but not forgotten. I had become engaged to be married some months before the end of the program to Irene, who came from a Polish family. The Russians warned me to "beware of Slavic women."

We were married in April of 2000, almost a year after the end of the program. To my surprise, I received a certificate from Tupolev that said, in part:

"The given certificate is a confirmation of your ability to cope with all difficulties in extreme situations similar

on the character to flood, fire, earthquake, volcano eruption, marriage or family life."
And:
"Let us congratulate on your marriage. At last it happened! We congratulate your bride with a very good taste. We swear before her and before the God, that she has chosen the very reliable man to herself as a husband."

This certificate was presented to me by my directorate chief during an awards ceremony. He said, in his Southern drawl, "Well, we sent a crackerjack instrumentation engineer to Russia and he returned as A-number-one marriage material."

The certificate, despite or because of being presented with tongue in cheek, proved to me that I had been successful in more than just helping to complete a program that broke the sound barrier — I had successfully broken a cultural barrier.

My perception of the world would never be the same.

# Pictures

St. Basil's Cathedral on Red Square

Dinner with Professor Poukhov (left, facing) and his wife (seated next to him). I am seated on her left. Michael Melnichenko is in right profile on the left.

Taking "stock" of my situation at Williamsburg, Virginia

In our Paris hotel. Left to right: Sergei Karabonov, Alexander Sudakov, Lyudmila, me, and Mr. Sablev.

Typical winter day in Moscow. I am on the left, next to my interpreter, Vladimir Merinov.

Left to right-The two American pilots of the Tu-144LL: Rob Rivers and Gordon Fullerton, Sergei Borisov (Tupolev pilot), Edgar Krupienski (Tupolev Chief Engineer), Alexander Pukhov (Tupolev Chief Designer)          NASA EC98-44749-30

Left to right: Mr. Sperny, me, and Mr. Sablev.

Onboard the Tu-144LL (left to right): Russ Barber, Robert Witcofski, Vyatcheslav Savin, me, and a Tupolev employee.

Cockpit of the Tu-144LL

Cold lunch at Zhukovsky. Donna Gallaher is on the left. Keith
Harris is on the right.

The Russian crew at Zhukovsky. Note the elegant snack laid out
on the table.

Group photo. Steve Rizzi is in the Purdue T-shirt. Donna Gallaher is to his left. Keith Harris is behind him. I am in the back row wearing glasses. Alexander Sudakov is on the far left. Michael Melnichenko is the man nearest to him. Boris Mirimov is on the far right.

Left to right: Vladimir Merinov, Boris Mirimov, Mr. Sperny, Sergei Borisov, me, Edgar Krupienski, Alexander Sudakov, Professor Poukhov

Tu-144LL at takeoff — showing canards deployed and nose droop                                    NASA EC97-44203-3

Tu-144LL making a low pass in "clean" configuration
NASA EC98-44749-23

Ishmylova flea market in Moscow

Winter in a Moscow Park

Moscow Metro station

A gift to me from the Russian team with their pictures and signatures on it. Marina Generalovna is in the center.

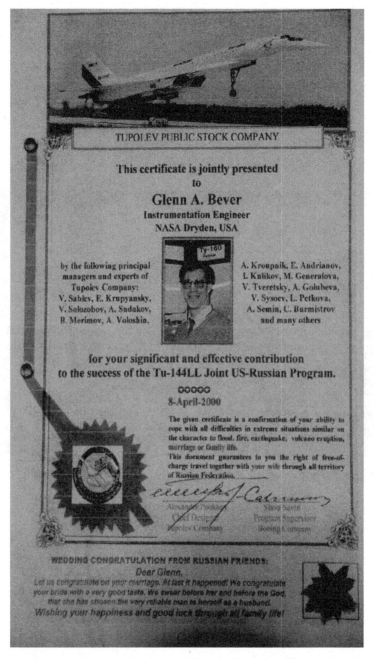

A wedding congratulations certificate from Professor Poukhov — tongue in cheek

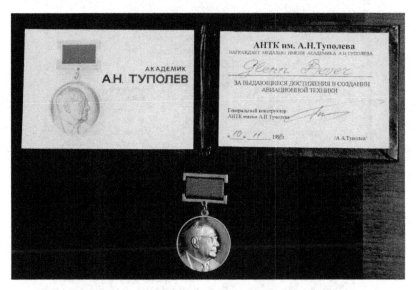

The medal awarded to me by Tupolev

I am stepping into the F-15D for Mach 2 flight

NASA AFRC2016-0168-04

# Part 2: Other Travails

# Chapter A
# The Grand Tou

Over the course of my career, I made many trips overseas, which of course led to often unexpected adventures. Some of these trips were tied to my Russian travel, but many were not. When they were tied together on the same excursion, you could experience the different cultures back-to-back.

## AGARD

From 1990 until 2006 I was a member of a group, operating under the auspices of the North Atlantic Treaty Organization (NATO), whose mission was to produce two series of volumes on flight test techniques and flight test instrumentation. I use the term "group" because throughout the years its name changed to fit the organization it was under. Here are some of the names the group went by: Working Group 11 (WG-11), Flight Test Technology Team (FT3), Flight Test Technical Team, Flight Test Technology Committee, etc. The "Advisory Group for Aerospace Research and Development" (AGARD) had existed for nearly 50 years under the auspices of NATO. My group operated under AGARD until 1997, when AGARD and the Defence Research Group (DRG) reformed into the Research and Technology Organisation (RTO). My group "re-formed" under RTO, but we had to spend an enormous amount of time explaining to our higher judicatory just what we did and why we continued to exist. Most of the AGARD groups formed to produce a particular volume and then disbanded. We, however, had produced (by the time I left the group) over 40 volumes and had several more in the pipeline. This did not fit their

zational model, so we had to keep pounding the square
g into the round hole in order to continue our work. They
didn't exactly want us to go away, but wouldn't let us exist as
we were. After many presentations and explanations, they would
still scratch their heads, grudgingly let us continue, and then
the cycle would start all over again when new delegates would
populate the boards or the umbrella organization would re-form.
(RTO subsequently has re-formed again into the Science and
Technology Organization, or STO.)

My first involvement with AGARD was in 1984 when I
wrote a paper that was accepted for presentation at a conference
in Lisbon, Portugal. While there, and feeling good about
presenting my paper in such a setting, I was pulled aside by the
WG-11 group. They talked me into writing an "AGARDograph"
(the name of the series of technical volumes)[1] to be co-authored
by a German author. Sometime later this author bowed out and
I was left as the sole author, which was unfortunate because
part of the reason for authoring this series was to combine best
practices and lessons learned on both sides of the Atlantic.

After two fact-finding trips in 1986 and 1987, I wrote
*Digital Signal Conditioning for Flight Test*,[2] which I finished
in 1990. That year I joined WG-11 as a member and took on
the role of technical editor, eventually writing the process by
which such volumes should be produced. The group included,
on the average, membership from 10 NATO countries — plus
Sweden, the site of my last European trip to attend a team
meeting (2006).

---

[1] AGARD, RTO, and STO AGARDographs: https://www.sto.nato.int/
pages/systems-concepts-and-integration-ft3.aspx

[2] Bever, Glenn A., *Digital Signal Conditioning for Flight Test*,
AGARDograph no. 160, vol. 19, 1991.

Over the next 16 years, I traveled typically twice a year to meetings with the group, usually in Western Europe. From 1995 to 1999 I sometimes combined these trips with my Russian visits. I made nearly 50 trips to Europe and visited 17 countries there.

### *Das ist mein Koffer* — Germany

It was the spring of 1987 and I was making my second trip to Europe. This was to be a month-long adventure taking me to several countries; Germany was my first stop. The first time I came to Europe (Portugal in 1984) my luggage was left in New York. My luck, being consistent, allowed it also to happen on this trip. I arrived in Hanover and waited for my luggage. While waiting, I met a driver that my hosting organization, DFVLR, had arranged. He did not speak English, so we waited in silence for a while. When it became obvious that the luggage wasn't going to appear, I went to the desk and they filed the information. The driver drove me, sans luggage, at over 100 miles per hour to Braunschweig and a "hotel" at the airport there. This "hotel" had the airport control tower on the top and a restaurant on the bottom — with a few floors in the middle tricked out as hotel rooms. So here I was, tired, somewhat cranky, and uncertain what to do next. The airlines had told me my baggage would be delivered to the hotel, but given the setup here I wasn't sure how the connection would be made. So I spent a good deal of time staring out the window hoping to spot my luggage arriving, and practicing the German phrase for "that is my suitcase." I finally gave up and went down to the restaurant where they handed me a menu — in German. This was not a tourist area. I was prepared to just point to something at random and give it a go, but the waitress — presumably recognizing my bewilderment — went over to another table and asked a patron to come over and translate the menu for me! He came over, sat opposite me, and proceeded to go through the menu, explaining to me what each item was. So I ordered, considerably less randomly than I would otherwise have had to do. This incident did much to turn my mood around.

The next morning I walked down to DFVLR, which was just down the street. After spending the day there I went back to the hotel and waited for my luggage again. Eventually, a car pulled up and delivered a suitcase I recognized to be mine. I ran downstairs and, pointing, proclaimed *"Das ist mein Koffer,"* which was apparently adequate for reclaiming my luggage. Reunited, I was much happier to continue with my European tour.

## Italy

While driving through Northern Italy I encountered a stoplight that had both the red and green light on at the same time. Several miles later I cautiously passed through another such light. After the third light like this, I really began to wonder what that meant, so at the next stop on my technical tour, I asked my host about it.

"What does it mean when a traffic light has both the red and green lights on at the same time?" I asked him.

"It means the traffic light is broken," he replied.

As I approached the Italian city of Cirea, where my contacts at Aeritalia had arranged a hotel for me, the first thing I noticed was the overall "sameness" of the place. Everything was the same color — an adobe tan. All the buildings looked the same to me, and I had no idea where to go. I had been given the hotel name and address but no directions to it and could not see any street names.

*My God,* I thought, *How am I ever going to find the place?*

In this time before cell phones, much less cell phones with GPS, I entered the town and started driving around looking for inspiration. I finally did the unthinkable; I stopped to ask directions. That is not as trivial as it sounds, however. I was in a smallish town in Italy and any directions I got were likely to be in Italian, a language I did not speak.

In my meanderings I had passed an establishment emblazoned with the name "American Bar and Grill." Well, that seemed like a good place to start. So I stopped and asked where I could find the hotel. No English spoken at the American Bar and Grill. Darn. So I pulled out a slip of paper with the hotel name on it and pointed questioningly. I have found this technique to be generally effective in letting people know what I need, and so it was here.

Everybody got into the act. Lots of chatter and hand motions. One word stood out to me. They kept referring to a *semaforo* where, according to the hand gestures, I was to turn left. Finally, someone drew a map, of sorts, and they felt their job was done.

I drove off, somewhat perplexed, but not knowing what else to do. However, I soon came to a stoplight (perhaps the only one in the village) and the light dawned, so to speak. *Semaforo* was a stop light — as in *semaphore* or *signal*.

I had learned — at least I thought I had learned — that I must make a left at the stoplight and then follow the "map." So I did, while peering at the sameness of everything. Against all odds I did find the hotel, noting that even sitting right in front of it I would have been hard pressed to know it *was* a hotel. I don't remember seeing a sign. If there was one it was quite small. The building itself looked practically deserted with a bombed-out look. Not promising.

Sighing, I went inside and found a check-in counter. Sure enough, it was the right place. Going to my room, I decided that it was adequate, but I noticed there was no lock on the door. In fact, the door barely closed. So I took my most valuable possessions with me as I went looking for a place to eat. There was a restaurant in the hotel, and upon entering it I was shocked. It was gorgeous. The tables were tricked out with starched white tablecloths. The crystal on the tables looked opulent. The waiters and other staff were well dressed. In short, it looked like a top-flight establishment. It was quite a contrast with the outside — and my room.

I later learned that due to the tax structure in Italy, a dilapidated exterior was not uncommon, because tax rates were based on exterior appearance. Interior appearance was apparently not considered for taxes. So the old saying "you can't judge a book by its cover" was particularly true here.

Upon returning to my room I moved a piece of furniture across the unlocked door and went to bed.

When I checked out of this hotel, it was on a holiday (May 1) — and the clerk on duty at the desk was not the "A" team. As he did not speak English nor I Italian, our communication was difficult. Further, they did not accept credit cards. Cash only, and I did not have enough Italian lira to pay the bill. I did have enough traveler's checks — in U.S. denominations — to cover the bill, but it became apparent the clerk did not know how to convert them to the Italian lira equivalent. I fished out a receipt I had for exchanging traveler's checks at the airport, and he started tentatively punching buttons on a calculator. Finally, he threw up his hands, turned his calculator around, shoved it to me, and gestured that I should do the conversion. So I did, and gave him what I hoped was the appropriate amount.

My currency troubles were not over. When I attempted to drive across the border from Italy into France a few days later, I found I had been on a toll road. So I fetched up at a toll booth, and there, once again, I had a currency problem. I did not have enough Italian currency on me, and I had not converted any to French currency yet. In these days before the Euro, one had to constantly be changing currency when traveling around Europe.

I was boxed in — literally. I looked behind me and there were several cars queued up. In front of me was the gate barring my way forward into France. I couldn't back up and I couldn't go forward due to my lack of correct currency. In desperation I handed the toll booth operator U.S. dollars. He wasn't happy about it, but he was forced to accept my payment. For my part, I didn't quibble about exchange rate. I was just relieved to see the gate arm rise, and I escaped into France.

## Goat Cheese, Anyone?

I had arranged my book "fact-finding" tour to include the WG-11 meeting that was being held near Marseilles, France, as they oversaw my activity. They were, in essence, my publisher.

I joined the group for dinner at a very pleasant restaurant in the South of France. I was sitting next to Tony Pool, who was from the Netherlands, so I figured that my best move was just to order what he did, as I had no knowledge of most of the items on the menu.

When the meal arrived it turned out that I had ordered warm goat cheese. I took my first bite and the expression on my face must have been a sight to behold. It was *awful*. But it was my dinner and I was hungry, so I steeled myself and took another bite. No improvement.

About that time Tony, who was busily eating his order looked over at me and exclaimed "I think we made a wise selection, don't you?"

I didn't, but I mumbled something and ate no more.

Ordering food in another country is often problematic. Reading the menu is the first obstacle. *Understanding* the menu is the second. Unfamiliarity with the food is the third. The least stressful way of ordering is to go to a cafeteria-style restaurant where you can see the food and just point to it. The total is rung up on a cash register and you can see the amount. If you are able to use a credit card, you don't even have to deal with change. (Credit card use in Europe wasn't common at that time.) Bing, bang, boom. You have recognizable food and minimal interaction with vendors who don't understand English.

However, sometimes even that doesn't quite work out. Once I was in an Italian sandwich shop and ordered a sandwich. The girl behind the counter asked me a question — in Italian — that I did not understand.

*"Per qui?"* she asked.

I shrugged and looked blank.

*"Per qui? Per qui?"* she asked again, more loudly each time.

Now I was beginning to sweat. I probed my memory banks for inspiration.

*"Per quiii!?"* she intoned again looking very agitated. As her frustration level rose and she kept repeating her question, the light finally dawned. I knew that *Por aqui* in Spanish means "for here." I guessed that the Italian words were similar. She was asking me if I wanted the sandwich "for here" (as opposed to "to go").

Experiences like that have sensitized me to poor user interfaces in the United States — such as pumping gas when the gas pump keeps asking irrelevant questions (do you want a car wash?) or questions that you have to think about the "sign" of the answer ("is this a debit card — yes or no" versus "is this a credit card — yes or no"). I think of the poor foreigner trying to navigate what they think are simple transactions only to be bombarded with questions they don't understand and didn't expect to have to answer.

## French Gendarmes

Driving through a town in central France, I was looking for the hotel where I was to stay. Most of the places I stayed were arranged by my local contacts and were usually not typical tourist hotels. This was good in that you experienced more of the local color, but the downside was that these hotels were often more difficult to find. While driving through the town a couple of times and seeing no sign of the hotel, I *had* seen a couple of French motorcycle policeman (*gandarmes*), so I finally stopped to ask directions. They did not speak English, but I used my tried and true technique of showing them a piece of paper with the hotel name on it and looking quizzical. They looked at it and then motioned for me to follow them. So it was that I got a police motorcycle escort through town. They finally pointed out the hotel to me and continued on their way. I have often heard people disparage the French, saying how impolite they are, but I have to say in all the times I have visited France, both urban and rural, I have never had a bad experience with them. I think that if you make even the smallest effort to communicate in the local language, people tend to bend over backward to help you.

## Missing the Train in Switzerland

Switzerland is famous for efficiency. A symbol for efficiency is that trains run on time. On one trip I had two reasons to be in

209

Europe that were a week apart. It was not worth returning home for that short period, so I got authorization to stay and take leave, which gave me a wonderful opportunity to do some touring. I took a train from Paris to Switzerland — stopping at Geneva and Bern and then on to Vienna, Austria. At one stop in Switzerland I had to change trains. I found out what train to get on and then went and sat in the train. It was on the track and I was way early. However, as time went on and the departure time got closer I noticed that nobody seemed to be getting on the train. I got more nervous. When the departure time passed I knew that something was wrong. So I finally got off the train and enquired at the ticket agent's booth. What I learned was that I was waiting on the wrong train. Further, the train I wanted had departed on time. Great. Now what do I do? The next train to where I wanted to go wasn't for several hours and it was not an express.

As it turned out, this was probably for the best. Since my travel plans were open and I did not have pre-set reservations anywhere, my schedule was very flexible. So this "setback" merely gave me more time at this stop, and the "milk run" train gave me a view of life in Switzerland that I wouldn't have otherwise seen. For example, we stopped a couple of times in the countryside (where there was no train station) to drop off children on their way home from school.

**Austria**

One of my favorite cities in Europe turned out to be Innsbruck, Austria. It was the site of a number of winter Olympic games and some of the Olympic infrastructure remained, such as the ski jump. I ran across a bell museum and learned a lot about bell manufacturing throughout the ages. The most charming experience was wandering around town and running into groups of children who were singing in the town plazas. There was a singing competition going on in town and in their free time they were entertaining the townspeople. There was another National Geographic moment when I ran across a small park with nearly life-sized chess pieces and a group of old men playing chess with them. I loved the small river running through the town of Innsbruck and a small tram that you could take to a little zoo on the other side. All told it was a very pleasant interlude.

When the train pulled into Vienna, Austria I was standing there trying to figure out my next move. A man approached and offered to rent me his apartment, which wasn't far from the train station. It was much cheaper than any hotel I could find and I decided to take him up on it. It turned out to be a good move. It was centrally located, and there was a small grocery store a block away where I could buy my own food and then cook it in the apartment — another savings. Vienna history is long, and I visited Beethoven's home, Mozart's grave, and attended a Mozart concert where the musicians were dressed in period costumes and using period instruments, like a harpsicord. A CD I bought there reminds me of that live performance to this day.

## Munich Hotel

One night my train went through Munich, Germany, and I decided to spend the night there. It was late and I didn't want to go very far, so I asked at the station information desk about local hotels and was directed to one just a block or so away from the train station. The place was, shall we say, seedy, but I was tired and took a room there. It turned out that my room was directly above a strip club and the bump and grind music kept me awake for half the night. Not much of a bargain.

# Chapter B

# Other Encounters

## Medical Treatment Overseas

I never had occasion to sample the medical treatment system in Russia, fortunately, as I never had the need. However I have seen it at work in other countries. One time when my wife and I were staying in Turin, Italy, she burned herself and had to seek medical attention. We went to a hospital a few blocks away from our hotel. Nobody spoke English. We tried Spanish and Russian, which I speak somewhat. We tried German and Polish, which Irene speaks. We even threw in a little French.

No dice.

I could understand enough Italian to hear them in the next room exclaiming that here we speak all these languages — but no Italian! Finally they unearthed a doctor who spoke English and he treated her. Upon leaving the examination room we looked around in confusion.

"What are you looking for?" the doctor asked.

"The place to pay," we said.

"Italy has socialized medicine. You don't pay," he said. "That's why I want to move to America."

I was travelling around Spain in 1990 and visited Seville, which was preparing for the World's Fair. After getting off the train, I went to a booth to ask the information agent something and then stood a short distance away trying to figure out where I was going to stay. The information agent I had just talked with approached me with an offer to sublet his apartment for a few days.

"I'm trying to save money so that I can get married," he said.

It was a good deal. Just like my experience in Vienna, it was an Air BnB years before there was such a thing.

That night I made a big mistake: After I got to the apartment I was too tired and lazy to go back out and search for a store in which to buy some bottled water, which I usually do.

So I drank the tap water in the kitchen.

I paid for it by spending the next couple of days holed up in the apartment in considerable gastric distress. I was miserable. Any plans I had for touring the city went by the wayside.

After a few days, my "landlord" — the information booth guy — came by to check on how things were going at his apartment.

I explained my predicament and he said "I can help you."

He pulled out a pad and wrote me a prescription for Imodium, directing me to a pharmacy a few blocks away. I was a little perplexed. Why was an information agent writing me a prescription? So I asked him, carefully, about that.

"I am a medical doctor," he told me to my astonishment.

"Why are you working in an information booth?" I asked.

"Because the pay is better," he said.

I did get out the next day to look around Seville.


On a plane to Germany some years later, my wife, who had just had a surgery that removed a small chunk of skin from her back, had the stitching pop open. So when we got to our destination in Germany — a small town — we were directed to a dermatologist there. The doctor didn't speak English so Irene got a workout of the German she had gained as an exchange student in Germany years before. Each day we would visit the doctor to check on her progress and each day she would ask about payment; and they said "We'll figure it out at the end of your treatment." The last day came and it was time to settle up. They shuffled some papers and then threw up their hands.

"It's free," they proclaimed. It was too much trouble to figure out how the insurances all worked.

So in Italy, Spain, and Germany we received free medical care, either by law or by insurance complications or by accident. The doctors, however, didn't necessarily fare so well.

I was visiting my physician cousin David in Florida. His wife was a nurse, and she had been to a medical conference in St. Petersburg, Russia. A doctor she met there gave her a medical paper that he wrote — but it was in Russian. She gave it to me and asked me if I could translate it for her.

"Probably not," I told her, "But let me give it a shot."

I was on my way to Russia at the time, so I took it with me and worked on translating it in my spare time. I was sitting in a conference room at Tupolev scratching my head over it when my interpreter, Michael, came in and asked me what I was doing.

"I'm trying to translate a medical paper for my cousin's wife," I told him.

"Give it to me. Let me try," he said.

With some relief I did so, and he returned with the translation a few days later.

"I had to buy two medical dictionaries," he said.

It gave him an excuse to buy them, I knew. He loved dictionaries.

With a twinkle in his eye, he proceeded to start reading the original Russian paper out loud to other Russians in the room.

They howled with laughter.

Puzzled, I asked Michael, "What's so funny?"

Chuckling, he said, "The paper is so full of medical jargon that even the Russians can't understand the Russian."

## Cultural Norms

We often are clueless regarding what we are clueless about when visiting foreign countries. We get so used to the way things are "done" at home that we don't stop to consider what might be done differently. Sometimes the simplest things cause us to scratch our heads.

Take flushing the toilet, for example. On more than one occasion I have had to hunt around to find out how a toilet flushed. I never expected the flusher to be a pull cord dangling above my head — but that is where I sometimes found it. Or finding reverse gear on a car. I have seen so many variations on this that the first thing I do upon renting a car in Europe is to locate reverse gear. Once, when renting a car in France, I gave up and drove 60 miles to my hotel, entered the parking garage beneath it, put the car in neutral — and pushed my car into a parking space. I then asked a colleague where the reverse gear was on that car.

"Oh, you pull up a ring on the gear shift," I was told.

When we traveled to other countries for the AGARD meetings, we typically had a host in that country — usually one of our members. This worked best. We had a guide, access to office "machinery," and someone who could plug us in to activities, tours, etc. On a few occasions, however, we met in places selected because the panel meeting of the group that oversaw our activities was meeting where we had no member stationed nearby. This happened in Norway. It also happened in Spain, where our team chairman, in order to be efficient, scheduled a meeting start time at what he felt was a reasonable hour — 8 a.m. What he failed to realize, however, was that *nobody* opened at 8 a.m. in Madrid. We got to our meeting spot and it was still closed.

In the Mediterranean region — particularly Spain — the typical work schedule is somewhat different from what Americans are used to. Work often starts at 9 or 10 a.m. Lunch/ siesta is about 2–5 p.m. and work continues until about 7 p.m., and dinner starts around 11 p.m. Good luck finding a restaurant open for business at 7 p.m.

## Languages

In addition to the Russian training at the Defense Language Institute, I had studied Spanish in school for some years and had become relatively fluent. Being a romance language, it gave me a leg up in being able to make some sense out of Italian, Portuguese, and French. With all of my travels, I collected a whole shelf full of translation dictionaries and travel guides. As I was usually traveling by myself, I could often blend in with the populace. I wouldn't give myself away by speaking English, since I had no companion to talk to.

I always tried to learn some of the language of the country I visited. I found that learning a half a dozen words to be mandatory: "where is?" "how much?" "thank you," "please," "excuse me," "hello," and "goodbye." With those words, a piece of paper, and pointing, much could be accomplished.

People generally appreciate you making the effort to speak their language, and they cut you a lot of slack.

## Mexico

In 1988 I traveled to Mexico City with a church group. We were there first to gain a better understanding of the conditions that poor people experienced there and secondly, to do some volunteer work. For the first few days we attended lectures by a Mexican professor who instructed us on Mexican history and culture. We were even invited to a Mexican wedding reception. That was fun.

Then it got more intense. We went out to the slum shanty towns surrounding Mexico City. Here people were living in cardboard and plywood "houses" slapped together. There was some electricity being used, but everyone ran their own lines from the power poles and the spider web of wires made my electrical engineering heart cringe.

We were invited into one of the clapboard homes, and sitting on the floor we were treated to Mexican hospitality. They brought in a case of bottled Pepsi for us to drink. They wanted to give us something that we were familiar with and would trust — because the bottles were sealed.

We were caught in a dilemma. On the one hand, we didn't want to drink a beverage that we knew cost them much more than they could afford. On the other hand, we didn't want to offend them by refusing their hospitality. It was a humbling experience. In the end we accepted the Pepsis, thankfully.

They seemed genuinely happy to see us and talk with us. I felt like a long-lost relative they had just discovered.

As we were preparing to leave, one of them jokingly asked, "So when are we going to be able to visit your homes?"

It was a sobering and embarrassing moment because we knew that was very unlikely to happen.

Later we went out to the countryside to visit a pueblo. From such a location, many *campesinos* left to pursue jobs in the city. Land distribution issues prevented many from making a living in the country. By now many of us were itching to *do* something, and when we discovered that they were digging ditches to lay in a water system, we eagerly grabbed picks and shovels and started helping.

I think they were amused at the sight of these unskilled *gringos* setting to with such vigor, and many of them leaned on their shovels and grinned knowingly. Meanwhile, the women were in the cooking hut preparing a meal — but the hut had no smokestack and the hut was filled with smoke. That couldn't have been healthy, but overall the surroundings were more pleasant than in the slums of Mexico City.

A phrase uttered by the Mexican professor came back to me. "In the countryside, we have poverty. In the city, we have misery."

## Poland

In 2005, my NATO Flight Test Technology Team (FT3) had a most unusual opportunity: We were to co-sponsor the first NATO meeting in Warsaw with the Society of Flight Test Engineers (SFTE). It was not only the first time we had a joint symposium with the SFTE, but it also was the first time a NATO symposium was going to be in Poland. It was surreal, having a NATO meeting in a former Warsaw Pact country. In fact, in Warsaw itself!

I actually went to Poland twice in support of this conference. The first time, Dan Roth, (our team chair) and I flew to Warsaw for a one-day meeting to plan the conference logistics. That was a grueling trip, especially for Dan, as he was experiencing some back pain. Traveling that far for such a short visit isn't ideal, but we felt it was necessary.

The second trip was for the conference itself, where I chaired a session. On that trip I took my wife, Irene, and three-year-old son, Sam. My wife's parents both emigrated from Poland following World War II and Irene spoke some Polish.

Her mother also joined us in Warsaw. She had not been back to Poland in 25 years.

Walking around Warsaw it was handy to have two Polish-speakers with me. However, on a few occasions we wanted Irene's mother to ask a stranger a question, but she was loath to do so. I discovered later that in speaking to a stranger she would be obliged to use "formal speech" in Polish, which she hated.

As a bonus, I got permission to take some vacation time following the conference and spent the next week touring Poland and visiting my wife's relatives. We first drove to Southwestern Poland and visited relatives on her mother's side. Her mother was with us on this part of the trip and that helped with introductions. We then drove on to the eastern part of Poland and the tiny town of Lędziny, where Irene's father was from, and visited relatives there. Sam, at three, was a great ambassador. Everybody loves a small child.

Following our trip to Poland, we asked Sam what part he liked best.

He said, "I liked the bus."

Of all the things we had done — flown through Paris to Warsaw, toured the country, chased pigeons in Krakow — the thing he remembered was riding the public transportation in Warsaw.

**New Zealand**

During a tour of the South Pacific in 1981, I spent a few weeks in New Zealand. Prior to traveling there, I had arranged for a "reciprocal operating license" so that I could use my Amateur Radio hand-held transceiver there. When I had moved to California from the Midwest, my Ham call letters changed to WD6ASL. When I traveled in New Zealand with a reciprocal license I would be using call letters assigned to that region, but I had to pick up the license at the Radio Inspector's office in Christchurch when I arrived.

However, my plane was late arriving from Australia. It was a Friday, and the Radio Inspector's office was closed for the weekend. I had planned to start touring the country the next day, and now it looked like I would have to go without my authorization to transmit.

I explained my dilemma to some helpful young ladies at the airport travel agency, and they suggested that I call the Radio Inspector at home; they even called around to find him and got him on the phone.

The Inspector offered to go back to his office, pick up my license, and personally deliver it to my hotel! I gratefully accepted his offer, and a while later he arrived at my hotel with his two young sons in tow, handed me the license — call sign ZL0ADL/WD6 — and then invited me to his house for dinner! (This happened to me again later in the New Zealand trip, when a local Ham operator drove down and invited me into his home.)

The Inspector's older, 11-year-old son was brimming with questions about the United States. The first thing he said to me was, "There's one thing I've been dying to ask an American. Are the highways in America really like they show on *Chips*?" He was referring to a popular American TV show of the period.

So right off the bat I experienced New Zealand hospitality from a government official who went out of his way to help me out. Dinner with his family was an experience that would not have happened if my travel had gone according to plan.

The next day I was to catch a tour bus, but we had a miscommunication and I waited for it at the wrong place, so I missed it. The hotel staff swung into action and arranged for me to take another bus to meet up with the first bus at their first stop on the tour. I spent the next week touring the beautiful countryside with a busload of Australians, a Japanese couple, two Canadians, and a few Brits. I was the only American. It was a delightful experience.

One of my fellow passengers was a large Australian who was travelling with his wife. He was very boisterous and excitable. He was enjoying his trip and I got the impression his boisterousness was typical behavior for him. His interactions were stereotypical of Australian enthusiasm.

One night we were sitting at dinner, which we ate communally, and he fixed me with a look. "You're awfully quiet for an American," he boomed. "Most Americans I meet are a lot louder."

His long-suffering wife looked embarrassed at her husband's declaration. I was chuckling inwardly, thinking that it was the pot calling the kettle black, so to speak. He was accusing Americans of being loud, when he himself was louder than just about anyone I had ever met. I told him, "Well, most Americans you meet are probably on holiday and are very excited." His wife jumped on that said, "Yes, dear, I'm sure that's how things are."

You don't have these sorts of conversations just bumping into people on the street.

One evening we had a talk and slide show by a 94-year-old photographer who has spent much of his life wandering around New Zealand by foot and mule. I thought he would be the ideal person to ask about the stars of the Southern Hemisphere, which were all new to me. His answer shocked me. "I never bothered to look up," he drawled.

When I flew to Auckland on the North Island of New Zealand, I attended a church service where I met the New

Zealand Deputy Minister of Finance and had a conversation with him. He was also the Minister of Communications and an Oxford Rhodes Scholar. Can you imagine touring Washington, D.C., having a bureaucrat drive down and open his office for you, invite you to dinner, and then running into the Secretary of the Treasury or FCC Chair and having a casual conversation?

I really liked New Zealand.

# Chapter C

# Trotting Along

## Bus Drivers and Catacombs of Rome

On a trip to Rome for a meeting, our host arranged a tour of the famous catacombs of Rome. Many people associate these subterranean passages with the persecution of early Christians, but they largely are burial grounds with sometimes elaborate sarcophagi.

An Italian Air Force bus picked us up and it was "escorted" by an airman on a motor scooter. Every so often the bus would stop and the motorcyclist would board and they would discuss, presumably, where to go next. It became obvious they did not know where they were going. Dutchman Rob Krijn and I both had maps and could see both where we were and where we had to go. However, our offers of help were rebuffed, so we spent way too much time in meandering to the catacombs. By the time we got there, they were nearly closed, but they allowed us in and we had a very nice tour. When we exited the catacombs and returned to the parking lot, the drivers were completely engrossed in studying the local map. *A bit late*, I thought.

On our way back to the hotel, our driver was exiting from a freeway, but then changed his mind. So he *backed up* on the off ramp in an attempt to continue down the freeway. Not surprisingly, we were rear-ended. The driver got out, filled out an accident report, and continued on. No big deal. He made it look like this happens every day — which by that point I was convinced it did.

## Turkey Trots

After one of our AGARD meetings in Ankara, Turkey, our host had arranged for a tour of central Turkey on a bus. We drove through an area that looked a great deal like the Mojave Desert where I lived. There was an area where the residents in past centuries had built catacombs to hide in when marauders rode through. We were slated to visit them. The night before this visit we were treated to dinner at a restaurant, which included entertainment by belly dancers. However, when I went to bed that night I got very sick from probable food poisoning. It was the most uncomfortable night of my life. I had several nightmares, sweats, fever, and nausea throughout the night. My room was next to a minaret where automatic calls to prayer were done — very loudly — at the appointed hours. It didn't help my already fractured sleep.

By morning I was much better and I was able to continue with the tour. There weren't many options. However, I discovered that squatting and duck walking through low-ceilinged catacombs is not an optimal position for dealing with residual diarrhea. When we finally emerged from the catacombs, I anxiously ferreted out a restroom — but was momentarily flummoxed by what I encountered there. It was a toilet where you squatted over a hole in the floor. Given my condition, I wasn't sure how to, shall we say, hit the target without soiling my clothes. I didn't ponder this question long, however, because of my state of urgency. I managed without incurring a cleaning issue and left greatly relieved.

## Scotland

It was quite pleasant driving through the Scottish countryside. The green hills and lochs were quite a change from the scenery back home in the desert. I had some days to kill between my meetings in England and an AGARD symposium in Edinburgh and took full advantage of it. I had a guidebook that listed several bed and breakfast places, and having selected one, I knocked on the door. An older woman answered it and appeared to be taken aback by my request to stay there. It became quite clear that she was uncomfortable with a single young man staying in her house. It had never occurred to me but admitting a lone stranger into her house must have conjured up all kinds of dangerous scenarios to her. She quickly closed her door and I was left to recover my aplomb and move on.

At the AGARD symposium in Edinburgh, we had a sumptuous dinner in a castle as a guest of the Lord High Mayor of Edinburgh. Following the reception a group of us went to a local restaurant which was tricked out in an American car theme. Bits of cars, bumpers, pictures, etc. peeked out of the walls. The contrast between the ancient Scottish castle and the American-theme restaurant was stark — and kind of disorienting.

## Amsterdam

Amsterdam is one of my favorite European cities. It is a wonderful city to walk around, full of small bridges and canals — and canal boats.

The Rijksmuseum had a large number of famous paintings by the masters — including *The Night Watch* painting by Rembrandt, which hung near the entrance to the museum. Van Gogh (pronounced "Fan Gohch" in Dutch, with the ending sounding like you are clearing phlegm from your throat) had a museum dedicated to his work.

I also found an engineering museum that celebrated all things engineering, particularly construction of dikes and bridges. It was one of the few places I encountered there where absolutely no signs were in English, which was an indication that it was off the beaten tourist track.

On one excursion I stumbled across the house where Ann Frank lived and in which she hid for a good part of World War II. Having read her diary it was an interesting — and sobering — place to visit.

The first time I arrived in Amsterdam, I was driving a rental car. There is *no place* to park in Amsterdam. I found my hotel and then spent considerable time driving all over looking for a place to park. Cars were parked next to the curb, *on* the street, and *on* the sidewalks. They were parked parallel. They were parked backed in. Every available space was filled with cars. As I was driving around, I spotted an office of my rental car's agency. I stopped there and asked if I could park my (their) car in their garage. They said yes! Problem solved.

Later, I retrieved my car from the garage to go for a drive around The Netherlands. I made sure I knew when the garage closed so that I would not get stuck with no place to park again. I spent a very pleasant afternoon driving around the countryside, visiting the Keukenhof gardens, a tulip market, the village of Beverwijk ("neighborhood of the Beavers" — of particular interest to me, given my last name), and various villages in Northern Netherlands that specialized in cheese-making.

My reverie was shattered, however, when I suddenly realized that time was getting away from me. I had to get back to the garage before it closed. Sweating bullets, I maneuvered the car back toward Amsterdam. I was driving by myself and didn't have time to stop and consult maps, so I "winged it." I pointed the car and drove — running on instinct. Miraculously, I arrived at the garage just as they were beginning to close the gate.

The Force was with me.

On another trip to Amsterdam, I was with the AGARD group. After business was done for the day, a favorite activity was to find an interesting restaurant and sample the local cuisine. However, it wasn't always the *local* cuisine that interested the group. On one occasion, they decided that we were going to the only Mexican restaurant in Amsterdam. It wasn't my first choice, since California is loaded with them and they held no particular fascination for me. *Because* California was well known to have many such restaurants, the group looked to me as the "resident expert" on what to order. I told them "It doesn't matter. It's all the same stuff: beans, rice, ground beef, and hot sauce."

The ambiance of the place was interesting. The walls were decorated with iconic Mexican beers — *Dos Equis* and *Corona* in particular. However, when it came time to order beer, the only one on the menu was *Heineken*. Not exactly in keeping with the Mexican theme.

## Luis's Merry Chase — Portugal

Professor Luis de la Costa Campos was a force to be reckoned with. He was well-read, well-traveled, well-respected, and spoke at least Portuguese, English, and German. He drove everywhere. He would drive from Germany to Portugal — or even Portugal to Turkey. His Land Rover vehicle was decked out with all kinds of (largely aircraft) instruments on the dashboard.

On one occasion he was hosting us during an AGARD meeting in Lisbon. Over the weekend he arranged to personally lead us on a tour of the Portuguese countryside. We all set off, blindly following him, and getting more perplexed as time went on. The countryside was beautiful, but we were heading, apparently, for the middle of nowhere — where we eventually arrived. In the middle of nowhere was a car repair garage, where

Luis was having a vehicle repaired. He had come to check on it — with all of us in tow! After he finished there we did have a very nice tour, visiting several nice areas, including Fatima, a pilgrimage site well known to Roman Catholics. It was a place where the Virgin Mary was reputed to have appeared to three shepherd children almost 100 years before. I was surprised when I looked down and saw people crawling past me. They were in a penitent position, moving toward the shrine.

## Partying in Spain

Flying to my first AGARD meeting as a member of Working Group 11 (WG-11), I found myself sitting next to an attractive Spanish woman. We were surrounded by other Spaniards and she was busy assisting them to get settled in. I had taken several years of Spanish, from junior high to college and decided to use the long flight from New York to Madrid to attempt actually speaking it. As what I had learned was Castilian Spanish, which is what is spoken in Madrid, I discovered that I understood more of what she was saying than if she were speaking, say, Mexican Spanish. Her name was Ana and she was a travel agent in Madrid. By the time we landed I had arranged a date with her. She came by my hotel and we had dinner together. Her English was pretty good — better than my Spanish — and we used both languages. I learned that she and some friends were leaving that weekend for the South of Spain, where her brother lived in Cordoba. I was planning to do some touring and ended up joining them for the first leg. We all took a train to Cordoba and upon arrival in late afternoon crashed at her brother's apartment for a siesta. We got up around 7 p.m. and went to a friend's house for a party, and then out to a street festival. We were up all night wandering around, eating at various booths, where families had set up to serve people, and had a great time.

Ana and I corresponded by mail after that trip and carried on a largely long-distance romance for a few years. She would write me in English and I in Spanish. We would correct each other's grammar and then return a copy. It was quite an incentive to improve our foreign-language skills.

# Closing Note

One of my goals when traveling is to make the trip as smooth as possible. As an engineer, I'm built that way — plan for the worst, have options, think ahead. But it frequently comes to pass that things don't go according to plan. When things go wrong, I remind myself that *this will make a good story someday* — and it helps me get through the experience. Travel is about adventure. Adventure is uncertainty. It is something different, and you encounter the unexpected. If you travel expecting to eat all the same foods you do at home, stay in hotels just like home, and not talk to the people living there, you might as well stay home and watch it on TV; it would be cheaper and less hassle — but you won't have the memories that stick with you and you won't stretch your perspective.

Something I struggled with was my propensity for staying put. Physicists call that *inertia* — the part about a body at rest tending to stay at rest. Travel is tiring. Making connections, finding somewhere to eat, where to get water, how to communicate, how to use the local money … is tiring. Adrenaline only takes you so far before you collapse. Once I got in the "safety" of my lodgings, I was often loath to bestir myself to go out. I often had to force myself to do that. *I'm here,* I would think, *I'm in a foreign country and have the opportunity to see things I may never have a chance to see again. Get up and explore!*

That said, I did have a policy of resting when I was tired. I saw no value in forcing myself to stay awake in an attempt to accelerate re-syncing my internal clock to the local time — which was often between 8 and 11 hours different from where I started a trip. Arriving overseas during the weekend and having a few days to ensure that I was up on my rest was something I tried to do whenever possible. There was one time I tried to violate that principle and planned to get off the plane from California on Monday and pretty much go straight to work in Moscow, but Tupolev outsmarted me and scheduled the first meetings for Tuesday. They were right, of course. You need all your wits about you in a foreign setting and sleep deprivation doesn't achieve that.

I am glad that I accepted the assignments and glad that I overcame my inertia in order to explore. It enriched me. It educated me. It gave me new perspectives and memories that I treasure — and I look forward to other adventures.

# Afterword

While this book is primarily about my experiences in Russia on the Tu-144LL program — and some other travels and NASA projects — my memoir would not be complete if I didn't mention the last couple of decades.

In 2002, my son Sam was born, and Irene and I have taken great pleasure in watching him grow. Seeing the world through his eyes has been delightful and instructive. He is now 16 years old and with each passing day I see that the world will be in good hands as he and his friends grow into adulthood. He is more capable than I ever was, but I relive my own joy at learning new things as I watch him attack life. His compassion and sensitivity combined with his intelligence are a killer combination. I want to be like him when I grow up.

My wife, Irene, has had to put up with a husband who gets distracted by shiny objects. I appreciate her forbearance more than she will ever know.

The many talented people at NASA I have had the pleasure of working with over the decades have made my professional life rich and fulfilling. My last boss at Armstrong, Brad Flick, has said "It is a blessing and a curse having so many bright people working for us." The curse is trying to direct a group of innovators who often have the right ideas but little patience for process, and the blessing is that they know how to get the job done — and redefine the process when needed. I was truly humbled as a supervisor to see the talent of the engineers working for me. Their accomplishments made me look good, even though my job was often just to get out of their way or run interference.

So as we move more firmly into the 21st century I see many more adventures ahead, and I look forward to another generation tackling solutions to the problems that their forbears have either created or let slide. There is always more work to be done — and always more fun to be had doing it.

# Appendix A

## *Russian Cyrillic Alphabet:*

| Letter: | Pronounced: | Letter: | Pronounced: |
|---------|-------------|---------|-------------|
| А | ah | П | peh |
| Б | beh | Р | ehr |
| В | veh | С | es |
| Г | geh | Т | teh |
| Д | deh | У | ooh |
| Е | ye | Ф | ef |
| Ё | yaw | Х | ha |
| Ж | zhe | Ц | tseh |
| З | ze | Ч | cheh |
| И | ee | Ш | shah |
| Й | ekratkeye | Щ | stchah |
| К | ka | Ъ | (hard sign) |
| Л | el | Ы | ouee |
| М | em | Ь | (soft sign) |
| Н | en | Э | eh |
| О | oh | Ю | you |
|   |    | Я | yah |

# Appendix B

## *Russian numbers:*

| Number: | Pronounced: |
|---------|-------------|
| 1 | adin |
| 2 | dva |
| 3 | tree |
| 4 | cheteerey |
| 5 | pyat |
| 6 | shest |
| 7 | sevn |
| 8 | vocim |
| 9 | dyevet |
| 10 | dyecit |

# Appendix C

## *Russian travel phrases:*

1.  Hello                              zdrazvwiche (Здравствуйте)
2.  Goodbye                            do svidaniya (До свидания)
3.  Yes                                da (да)
4.  No                                 nyet (нет)
5.  Please                             pazhalsta (пожалуйста)
6.  Thank you                          spasiba (спасиво)
7.  Excuse me                          eezveeneetyeh (извините)
8.  Where is …                         gdyeh (где)
9.  How much …                         skulka stoheet (сколько стоит)
10. Check please                       schyot pazhalsta (счёт, пожалуйста)
11. I don't speak Russian.             Nye gavaryou pa-ruski.
    Only English.                      Tolko pa-angliski.

# Appendix D

## *Tu-144LL Flight Overview*

| Flight | Date | Takeoff Time (UTC) | Landing Time (UTC) | Supersonic Max Mach |
|---|---|---|---|---|
| 1 | 29-Nov-1996 | 10:54 | 11:37 | |
| 2 | 11-Dec-1996 | 09:14 | 10:31 | |
| 3 | 2-Apr-1997 | 12:18 | 15:13 | |
| 4 | 11-Apr-1997 | 10:28 | 13:55 | |
| 5 | 18-Apr-1997 | 08:05 | 11:58 | |
| 6 | 21-May-1997 | 07:42 | 09:02 | 1.41 |
| 7 | 30-May-1997 | 11:37 | 13:10 | 1.80 |
| 8 | 10-Jun-1997 | 08:25 | 09:49 | 1.98 |
| 9 | 8-Oct-1997 | 09:25 | 11:49 | |
| 10 | 29-Oct-1997 | 12:05 | 14:01 | 1.98 |
| 11 | 14-Nov-1997 | 09:14 | 11:11 | 1.80 |
| 12 | 19-Nov-1997 | 08:50 | 11:22 | |
| 13 | 24-Nov-1997 | 11:14 | 13:01 | |
| 14 | 11-Dec-1997 | 09:18 | 11:07 | |
| 15 | 19-Dec-1997 | 10:04 | 12:28 | 1.60 |
| 16 | 22-Jan-1998 | 09:58 | 12:04 | |
| 17 | 29-Jan-1998 | 10:41 | 12:45 | 1.98 |
| 18 | 5-Feb-1998 | 09:59 | 12:03 | 1.66 |
| 19 | 11-Feb-1998 | 10:47 | 12:23 | 1.97 |
| 20 | 8-Sep-1998 | 09:40 | 11:24 | |
| 21 | 15-Sep-1998 | 06:58 | 09:38 | |
| 22 | 18-Sep-1998 | 07:08 | 09:17 | 1.96 |
| 23 | 24-Sep-1998 | 06:58 | 09:39 | 1.97 |
| 24 | 22-Mar-1999 | 10:51 | 13:22 | |
| 25 | 30-Mar-1999 | 13:14 | 15:18 | 1.80 |
| 26 | 2-Apr-1999 | 08:12 | 10:02 | 1.99 |
| 27 | 14-Apr-1999 | 12:43 | 14:52 | 1.99 |

# Glossary

| | |
|---|---|
| AAEFA: | Army Aviation Engineering Flight Activity. The name of the U.S. Army flight test organization on Edwards Air Force Base. |
| Abbey, George: | Center Director of the NASA Johnson Space Center. |
| AC: | Alternating current. |
| ACTIVE: | Advanced Control Technology for Integrated Vehicles. A project on an F-15B aircraft that explored thrust vectoring of its engine exhaust nozzles. |
| Aeroflot: | Russian airline. |
| AGARD: | Advisory Group for Aerospace Research and Development — an organization that was part of NATO, charged with research and development and interchange of such information within NATO. |
| AGARDograph: | The name used for technical papers or volumes published by AGARD and subsequently by the RTO. |
| AICS: | Airborne Instrumentation Computer System. A microprocessor-based system developed by the author used in several NASA research aircraft. |
| AIFTDS: | Airborne Integrated Flight Test Data System. The name given to a data acquisition system developed for NASA that included the RCU, RMDU, and SATM. |
| AIMS: | Airborne Information Management System. A Transputer-based system |

| | |
|---|---|
| | developed by the author and his team and used in several NASA research aircraft. |
| Aldrin, Buzz: | Edwin Aldrin. NASA astronaut who became famous as the crewmate of Neil Armstrong when they were the first to land on the moon in the Apollo 11 mission. |
| AM: | Amplitude modulation. A mode of modulation used to transmit voice and music over radio. |
| Ames: | The NASA Ames Research Center in California. |
| Anders, William: | NASA astronaut and Air Force major general. He was part of the Apollo 8 crew that was first to orbit the moon. |
| Armstrong: | The NASA Armstrong Flight Research Center in California, where the author worked. It was previously named the Dryden Flight Research Center and the NASA Flight Research Center. |
| Armstrong, Neil: | A former NASA (Dryden) Flight Research Center research test pilot and engineer who later became famous as the first man to walk on the moon (in the Apollo 11 mission). The NASA Dryden Flight Research Center was renamed as the NASA Armstrong Flight Research Center in his honor. |
| ARRL: | American Radio Relay League. A national association dedicated to amateur radio. |
| Ashtech: | Company that manufactured the Z-12 GPS system used on the Tu-144LL project. |

| | |
|---|---|
| ATLAS: | Adaptable Target Lighting Array System. A system that provided ground targets of lights that turned on and off in pseudo-random sequences as a method of assessing aircraft handling qualities in an air-to-ground task. |
| avionics: | A contraction of "aviation electronics." |
| bandwidth: | The range of frequencies used in a transmission or the rate of data transfer. |
| Barber, Russ: | NASA Dryden project manager on the Tu-144LL program. |
| Beaulieu, Warren: | Rockwell propulsion engineer and manager. |
| Bennett, Don: | NASA Dryden Flight Research Center engineer. |
| Bever, Emily Frank: | Author's mother. |
| Bever, Glenn: | Author. |
| Bever, Joe: | Author's brother. |
| Bever, Robert: | Author's father. |
| Bever, Sam: | Author's son. |
| Bever (Moore), Theresa: | Author's sister. |
| bit: | A contraction of "binary digit." |
| Blackwell, George: | NASA (Dryden) Flight Research Center security chief. |
| Boeing: | Large aerospace company and prime contractor for the Tu-144LL program. |
| Borek, Bob: | NASA Dryden Flight Research Center engineer. |
| Borisov, Sergei: | Chief Tupolev pilot of the Tu-144LL. |
| Borman, Frank: | NASA astronaut and commander of the Apollo 8 mission — the first to orbit the moon. |

| | |
|---|---|
| Brown, Jerry: | NASA Ames research engineer. |
| calibration: | The process of observing and tabulating sensor or system outputs based on known inputs and using that information to create mechanisms for accurately determining what an unknown input is by observing the output. |
| Campos, Luis de la Costa: | Portuguese professor and member of AGARD WG-11 and RTO FT3. |
| Carpenter, Scott: | Second American astronaut to orbit the earth. After he left NASA, he participated in several Naval undersea projects. |
| Cessna 152: | A single-engine aircraft that holds two passengers. |
| Cessna 182: | A single-engine aircraft that normally holds four passengers. |
| chord: | On a wing, the line front to back at a given distance from the aircraft body. |
| Christiansen, Rich: | NASA Acting Associate Administrator of the Aeronautics and Space Transportation Technology Enterprise (at the time of his Moscow visit in support of the Tu-144LL project). |
| clear rails: | Keeping clear of the area where the cockpit canopy comes down and seals when being closed. |
| CoCom limits: | Limits defined by the Coordinating Committee for Multilateral Export Controls. Limits altitude and ground speed above which a GPS unit is not normally allowed to transmit information. |
| Cold War: | The standoff between the Soviet Union sphere and the United States |

and its allies that existed from the late 1940s until 1991, when the Soviet Union ceased to exist.

commutation:

The process of sampling different pieces of data and forming them into a serial data stream with known positions relative to synchronizing markers in the data stream.

Concorde:

Anglo-French designed supersonic transport aircraft — and rival of the Russian Tu-144.

co-op program:

Co-operative education program. A co-operative agreement between colleges and government or industry that allows college students to rotate between terms of academics and industry experience.

Cooper-Harper ratings:

Criteria used by test pilots to evaluate the handling qualities of an aircraft.

Cousteau, Jacques:

Jacques Yves-Cousteau was the inventor of SCUBA and captain of the RV *Calypso* research ship.

CW:

Continuous wave. Unmodulated radio. Turning on and off the radio signal is the method used to carry information using codes — such as Morse Code.

Cyrillic:

The alphabet used for the Russian language. It is similar to the Greek alphabet — having been developed by Greek brothers Cyril and Methodius in the ninth century C.E.

data acquisition:

The process of taking measurements and storing or transmitting the data.

decom:

Short for "decommutator."

decommutator:

A device that converts a serial telemetry data stream (that had been

|  | commutated) into its constituent data words. |
| DEEC: | Digital Electronic Engine Control. Also the designation for the project that used an F-15 to test such a controller on its engine. |
| Denver, John: | American pop singer and amateur pilot. |
| DePaul, Judith: | American head of IBP, which was a pass-through company on the Tu-144LL program and provided, among other things, interpreters and drivers to the American team. |
| DFVLR: | *Deutsche Forschungs- und Versuchsanstalt für Luft- und Raumfahrt.* German Test and Research Institute for Aviation and Space Flight. Predecessor to DLR. |
| DLI: | The Defense Language Institute in Monterey, California where the author first learned Russian. |
| DLR: | *Deutsche Forschungsanstalt für Luft-Und Raumfahrt.* German Center for Aviation and Space Flight. |
| DRG: | Defence Research Group — an organization that was part of NATO, charged with some of the research and development and testing for NATO. |
| Dryden: | The NASA Dryden Flight Research Center in California, where the author worked. It is now named the NASA Armstrong Flight Research Center. |
| Eagle departure: | Taking off from the runway and then pointing straight up to gain altitude very quickly. The F-15 has more thrust than drag even without lift provided by its wings. |

| | |
|---|---|
| EE: | Electrical Engineering. |
| EEPROM: | Electrically Erasable Programmable Read-Only Memory. A form of non-volatile memory (retains its contents when the power is turned off) that can be reprogrammed without being removed from the circuit. |
| eminent domain: | The authority that allows government entities the right to buy up private property to further public works — such as building a freeway — whether or not the property owners agree to sell. |
| Engle, Joe: | NASA astronaut who flew the X-15 and later some of the Space Shuttle approach and landing test flights as well as the second Shuttle space flight. |
| F-4 *Phantom*: | Supersonic jet fighter aircraft. |
| F-15 *Eagle:* | Supersonic jet fighter aircraft. |
| F-16XL: | A delta-wing version of the F-16 jet fighter aircraft. |
| F-18 *Hornet*: | Supersonic jet fighter aircraft. |
| F-104 *Starfighter*: | Supersonic jet interceptor aircraft. |
| FAA: | Federal Aviation Administration. |
| Farrah Fawcett Majors: | Famous American television actress. |
| FCC: | Federal Communications Commission. |
| FIFO: | First-in-first-out (memory). A way of allowing two asynchronous (no common timing) activities to exchange data, especially if the input bursts data at higher speeds than it outputs steadily. (It's like sporadically topping off a bucket of water that has |

a hole in the bottom — which streams steadily.)

Flick, Brad:
Director of Research and Engineering at the NASA Armstrong Flight Research Center.

FORTRAN:
Formula Translation. The name of a high-level computer language.

Franz, Nadja:
Interviewer for the German TV show *Konkordski*.

Fred:
The name given to a large, wooden-framed photograph of the Tu-144 given as a gift to Tupolev.

FRR:
Flight readiness review. A Dryden process for deciding whether or not an aircraft is ready to proceed with a flight or series of flights.

FT3:
NATO Flight Test Technology Team. A descendent of WG-11.

FTS:
Federal Telecommunication Service. A U.S. government telephone system.

Fullerton, Gordon:
NASA Dryden research test pilot and former NASA astronaut who flew some of the Space Shuttle approach and landing test flights and Shuttle space missions. He also flew the Tu-144LL.

Fulton, Fitz:
NASA Dryden research test pilot. Flew, among many others, the Shuttle carrier aircraft in the approach and landing tests and also the KC-135 Winglet aircraft that the author flew in.

g:
Unit representing the force of gravity. For example, "2 g" is twice the force of gravity on Earth.

Gallaher, Donna: NASA Langley technician who worked on the Tu-144LL cabin noise experiment.

Gates, Bill: Co-founder of Microsoft Corporation.

Generalovna, Marina: Tupolev engineer responsible for the temperature measurements on the Tu-144LL.

Gorbachev, Mikhail: The last leader of the Soviet Union before its collapse in 1991.

GPA: Grade point average. A measure of academic accomplishment.

GPS: Global Positioning System. Used in navigation to determine speed and position.

Grones, Royce: USAF test pilot. Was one of the KC-135 Winglet project pilots.

Haise, Fred: NASA astronaut who flew on the Apollo 13 mission and later flew some of the Space Shuttle approach and landing test flights.

Hale, Alan: Eastern Washington University professor and USAF test pilot.

ham radio: Amateur radio. Operators who pass electronic, regulatory, and (sometimes) morse code tests are assigned call letters and allowed to engage in two-way radio communication on a variety of defined frequency bands.

Harris, Keith: NASA Langley technician who worked on the Tu-144LL cabin noise experiment.

Heathkit: A manufacturer of electronic kits.

HF: High frequency. A term used to define the radio frequency region between 3 MHz and 30 MHz.

| | |
|---|---|
| Hoadley, Art: | Western Michigan University professor. |
| HP: | Hewlett-Packard. A manufacturer of computer and test equipment. |
| HUD: | Heads Up Display. An instrumentation display used in aircraft to keep pilot's head out of the cockpit and looking at the situation outside the aircraft. |
| Hughes, Wes: | NASA Dryden technician. |
| hypersonic: | Highly supersonic. Generally, speeds above Mach 5 are considered hypersonic. Above this speed, molecular dissociation and ionization become important. |
| hysteresis: | The phenomena whereby the direction of an input sweep impacts the output. E.g., going up in pressure yields a different output at a given pressure than going down in pressure through the same pressure point. |
| Hz: | Abbreviation for Hertz, a unit meaning cycles per second. |
| IBP: | IBP Aerospace Group Inc.—a British-based company headed by an American. (See Judith DePaul.) |
| Iliff, Ken: | NASA Dryden Chief Scientist. |
| inertia: | The principle in physics that states: "A body in motion tends to stay in motion. A body at rest tends to stay at rest." In other words, it takes energy to change the state of motion (speed and direction). |
| Intel: | Integrated circuit manufacturer. |
| Irene: | Author's wife. |
| IT: | Information Technology. |

jeton:

French word for *token* which was adopted by Russians. Used in the Moscow metro system to gain entry.

Jetstar:

C-140 executive jet. Converted by NASA to be a research aircraft.

Jobs, Steve:

Co-founder of Apple Computer, Inc.

Karabonov, Sergei:

Russian interpreter.

KC-135:

U.S. Air Force tanker used for in-flight refueling. Dryden refitted one to test the aerodynamics of winglets.

KGB:

Soviet intelligence agency.

Kilobyte:

1024 bytes (of memory, usually). Often approximated as 1000 bytes, but the term is related to the number of bytes addressable by 10 binary digits — which is 1024.

Knightkit:

The label used by Allied Radio Corporation for a series of electronic kits.

Krijn, Rob:

Member of NATO WG-11 and subsequently FT3.

Krupyanski, Edgar:

Tupolev chief of the Tu-144LL flight team.

Kuznetsov:

Russian design bureau for aircraft engines.

kvass:

Russian fermented drink commonly made from rye bread.

Langley:

The NASA Langley Research Center in Virginia.

LAX:

Los Angeles International Airport in California.

LLRV:

Lunar Landing Research Vehicle. This ungainly flight vehicle, sometimes referred to as the "flying bedstead," was developed to give Apollo astronauts experience with landing the Lunar Module on the Moon—while still on Earth.

| | |
|---|---|
| Losey, Lori: | NASA Dryden videographer. |
| Lowall, Ed: | Author's amateur radio mentor. |
| LSI-11: | A microcomputer board using a multi-chip large scale integration (LSI) technology. The LSI-11 used the same instruction set as the venerable PDP-11 minicomputer (made by the Digital Equipment Corporation, or DEC), from which it was descended. |
| Mach number: | The speed of an aircraft relative to the speed of sound in the region of flight. |
| Mallick, Don: | NASA Dryden research test pilot, who among many other things flew both the lunar landing research vehicle (LLRV) that simulated a lunar module and the C-140 Jetstar. |
| Marshall: | The NASA Marshall Space Flight Center in Alabama. |
| Matlab: | A computer language/script by Mathworks targeted at scientific and engineering analysis and modeling. |
| matryoshka: | Russian name for nested dolls. |
| McMurtry, Tom: | NASA Dryden research test pilot. Flew, among many others, the Shuttle carrier aircraft in the approach and landing tests; the KC-135 Winglet aircraft; the C-140 Jetstar; and the F-104 Starfighter that the author flew in. |
| Melnichenko, Michael: | Russian interpreter. |
| MHz: | Megahertz. One million cycles per second. |

MIL-STD-1553:            A standard data bus used on military aircraft to pass information between avionic subsystems.

Montgomery, Terry:      NASA Dryden engineer.

Morse Code:             A code that uses turning on and off a signal or light source to convey letters of the alphabet and other characters.

myelogram:              A medical procedure where dye is injected into the spinal column to provide a contrast allowing certain spinal abnormalities to show up on an X-ray.

NACA:                   National Advisory Committee for Aeronautics — the predecessor to NASA. Nobody in those days pronounced it as a word. They sounded out each letter when referring to it.

NASA:                   National Aeronautics and Space Administration. Notice the first "A" in NASA.

NATO:                   North Atlantic Treaty Organization.

Nimoy, Leonard:         Actor who is most famous for playing "Mr. Spock" on TV shows and movies.

NK-321 engines:         Russian engines manufactured by Kuznetsov for the Tu-160 "Blackjack" bomber that were retro-fitted into the Tu-144LL.

NT-33A:                 A jet aircraft trainer that was modified for use as an airborne simulator.

NTSC:                   National Television System Committee. The name used for the television analog broadcast format commonly used in the United States.

OCCAM:                  A computer language unique to the Transputer that was designed to intrinsically allow parallel processing. Its name was derived from "Occam's razor" which is a problem-solving principle stating that the simplest solution tends to be the right one.

Orion:
The name of the new NASA spacecraft designed for human deep space exploration.

OV-1 *Mohawk*:
U.S. Army aircraft used on a stall speed warning project.

PAL:
Phase Alternating Line. A television analog broadcast format found in countries that use a 625 line/50 fields per second broadcast — such as in Europe.

parallel processing:
Computers classically execute one instruction at a time. In parallel processing, multiple strings of instructions execute simultaneously.

Parikh, Pradeep:
Boeing deputy program manager.

PCB:
Printed circuit board.

PCM:
Pulse code modulation. A coding technique used in creating a telemetry stream.

per diem:
The daily travel pay to take care of travel costs. This varies depending on the area being traveled to.

peredniki:
Russian name for *aprons*.

Peterson, Bruce:
NASA Dryden research test pilot who, as a result of a spectacular crash landing, became somewhat famous when the crash was used in the opening scenes of a popular TV show.

photoreader:
A device that uses light sensors to read paper tape with holes punched in it. A hole represents a "one" and no hole represents a "zero."

| | |
|---|---|
| Pickering, Thomas: | U.S. Ambassador to Russia (1993-1996). |
| Piper Tomahawk: | PA-38-112. A single-engine aircraft that the author trained in when learning to fly. |
| piroshki: | Russian burrito-sized wraps containing different fillings — such as cabbage and meat. |
| Pool, Tony: | Dutch member of the NATO Working Group 11 (WG-11). |
| Poukhov, Alexander: | Tupolev Chief Designer. He headed the Tupolev effort to resurrect and fly the Tu-144LL. |
| Princen, Norm: | American handling qualities research engineer who worked for Douglas Aircraft. |
| QST: | The name of the ARRL magazine. The term was derived from the radio "Q" signal meaning "calling all stations." |
| Rackl, Robert: | Boeing engineer working on the cabin noise experiment. |
| ratiometric calibration: | For calibration purposes, using the ratio of the sensor output to the level of voltage powering the sensor instead of just using the sensor output alone. |
| RCU: | Remote Controller Unit. Controlled multiple RMDUs. |
| Rivers, Rob: | NASA Langley research test pilot who flew the Tu-144LL. |
| Rizzi, Steve: | NASA Langley lead experimenter for the Tu-144LL cabin noise experiment. |
| RMDU: | Remote Multiplexer Digitizer Unit. A programmable data acquisition system. |

| | |
|---|---|
| Rogers, Roy: | American actor/singer who played in many TV and movie westerns. |
| Rood, Rich: | NASA Dryden instrumentation engineer. |
| Ross, Jerry: | NASA mission specialist astronaut who tied the record for the number of launches into space — seven. |
| Ross, Jim: | NASA Dryden photographer. |
| Roth, Dan: | Chair of the RTO Flight Test Technology Team. |
| RTO: | Research and Technology Organisation — A descendent of both AGARD and DRG. Formed in a reorganization of NATO. |
| ruble: | Russian unit of monetary currency. |
| RV: | Research Vessel. A ship designation defining its mission. |
| Sablev, Vyatcheslav: | Mr. Sablev was a Tupolev manager. |
| SATM: | Stand Alone Timing Module. Allowed an RMDU to control the data acquisition process rather than rely on an RCU to control it. |
| SC-01 phoneme synthesizer: | An integrated circuit (chip) that contained addressable phonemes — or basic sounds — from which English words could be constructed. |
| Schob, Walt: | USAF test pilot — and the author's flight instructor. |
| SCUBA: | Self-contained underwater breathing apparatus. The compressed air tanks and regulators worn by divers. |
| Serial link: | Passing data one bit at a time (serially) between two devices. |
| SFTE: | Society of Flight Test Engineers. |
| Shafer, Mary: | NASA Dryden handling qualities engineer. |

| | |
|---|---|
| Sheremetyevo: | An airport serving Moscow, Russia. |
| Simpson, OJ: | American athlete charged with murdering his wife. |
| Smith, Dan: | Boeing program manager. |
| Smolka, Jim: | NASA Dryden research test pilot. |
| SOFIA: | Stratospheric Observatory for Infrared Astronomy. A converted Boeing 747SP aircraft containing a large infrared telescope used in astronomical observations. |
| Sperny: | Mr. Sperny was the head of the calibration lab at Tupolev's Zhukovsky site. |
| SR-71: | A high-altitude, high-speed reconnaissance aircraft used by the United States government — including NASA. |
| SSB: | Single side band. A radio modulation method used for efficient bandwidth of a voice channel, but is somewhat unstable. |
| static line: | A cord that connects a parachute to an aircraft so that when the parachutist jumps out, the connection opens the parachute by pulling it out of the pack as the jumper falls. |
| STO: | Science and Technology Organization—a descendent of NATO RTO. |
| STS-1: | The first Space Shuttle mission to launch into space. |
| Sudakov, Alexander (Sasha): | Tupolev chief instrumentation engineer on the Tu-144LL. |
| supersonic: | Speed in excess of the speed of sound. |
| Swan 350: | An amateur radio transceiver manufactured by Swan Engineering. |

| | |
|---|---|
| Szalai, Ken: | Center Director of the NASA Dryden Flight Research Center. |
| T-28: | Army single-engine training aircraft used as a chase plane by AAEFA. |
| TAS: | True Air Speed. The speed of the aircraft relative to the airmass in which it is flying. |
| TBI: | Tennessee Bureau of Investigation. |
| telemetry: | Transmitted data, usually from a remote location. |
| TF-104G: | A two-seat version of the F-104 *Starfighter*. |
| TLC: | The Learning Channel. A television network. |
| transceiver: | A radio that both transmits and receives. |
| transducer: | A device that converts a physical phenomena — like pressure, temperature, or acceleration — into an electrical signal that can be interfaced to a data acquisition system. |
| Transputer: | A 32-bit microprocessor with a unique architecture designed for parallel processing through networking with other Transputers via intrinsic high-speed serial links. |
| Truly, Dick: | NASA astronaut who flew some of the Space Shuttle approach and landing test flights and Shuttle space missions and subsequently became NASA Administrator. |
| Tu-144LL: | Russian Tu-144D supersonic transport aircraft modified by Tupolev. The "LL" designation stands for *Letayushchaya Laboratoriya* |

|  |  |
|---|---|
| | (Летающая Лаборатория), which is "flying laboratory" in Russian. |
| Tupolev: | Tupolev Design Bureau. An aircraft design and manufacturing company in Russia. They were responsible for the development of the Tu-144 and also the resurrection of the Tu-144LL. |
| U2: | A high-altitude reconnaissance aircraft used by the United States. |
| Vandiver, Wilson: | NASA Dryden instrumentation engineer — and author's predecessor on the Tu-144LL program. |
| Vnukovo: | An airport serving Moscow, Russia. |
| W0NIC: | Ed Lowall's amateur radio call letters. |
| WA0WFQ and WN0WFQ: | Author's former amateur radio call letters. |
| Wagner, Dave: | NASA Dryden contractor engineer. |
| WD6ASL: | Author's amateur radio call letters. |
| WG-11: | Working Group 11 — The AGARD working group charged with the publication of best practices for flight test instrumentation and flight test techniques. |
| Wilner, Doug: | NASA Dryden instrumentation engineer. |
| Wilson, Earl: | NASA Dryden chief of the instrumentation branch. |
| wind shear: | The sudden change in wind direction or intensity from one region of airmass to the next. |
| winglet: | An upswept appendage at the tip of a wing used to break up vortices that form there and reduce aerodynamic drag — which improves fuel economy. |

| | |
|---|---|
| Wozniak, Steve: | Inventor of the original Apple computers and Co-founder of Apple Computer, Inc. |
| X-15: | Hypersonic, rocket-powered test aircraft flown between 1959 and 1968, during which time the three aircraft made 199 flights. Several flights exceeded 50 miles in altitude — the official boundary above which pilots qualify as astronauts. Twelve men flew them, including Joe Engle and Neil Armstrong. |
| X-24B: | A wingless aircraft built to test the concept of using lift developed by the aircraft body. |
| X-29A: | An experimental jet aircraft with forward swept wings. |
| Zhukovsky Air Base: | The base of operations for the Tu-144 outside of Moscow, Russia — and where the Tu-144LL was modified and flown. |
| ZL0ADL/WD6: | Author's amateur radio call letters when travelling in New Zealand. |

# About the Author

Glenn Bever is a retired Deputy Director for Research and Engineering at the NASA Armstrong Flight Research Center, where he also previously served as Chief of the Flight Instrumentation and Flight Systems branches. He was project Chief Engineer for the F-18 Automated Aerial Refueling and the C-17 research flight computing system projects. For much of his 42-year career there he developed embedded systems for research aircraft ranging from an Army OV-1 propeller aircraft and a KC-135 tanker to supersonic fighters such as F-104 Starfighter, F-18 Hornet, and F-15 Eagle as well as SR-71 and Tu-144LL supersonic high altitude aircraft.

For 16 years Glenn was the NASA representative to the NATO Advisory Group for Aerospace Research and Development (AGARD) Flight Test Techniques Group responsible for publications about flight test techniques and flight test instrumentation. Glenn authored the AGARDograph publication *Digital Signal Conditioning for Flight Test.*

Between 1995 to 1999, Glenn spent much of his time in Russia representing the United States as instrumentation and on-site engineer for the Tu-144LL high speed research program, the subject of this book.

For his work, NASA has awarded Glenn with its Exceptional Engineering Achievement, Outstanding Leadership, and Exceptional Service medals. Although retired, Glenn holds a position as the first Emeritus engineer at NASA Armstrong.

Made in the USA
Columbia, SC
05 April 2019